COOKIES

for

Grown-ups

Cookies for Grown-ups

ISBN: 978-1-933176-42-0

Red Rock Press

New York, New York

www.RedRockPress.com

Design by Susan Smilanic

Studio 21 Design

Durango, Colorado

Library of Congress Cataloging-in-Publication Data

Cooper, Kelly, 1957-

Cookies for Grown-ups / Kelly Cooper ; with photographs by Frank Anzalone.

p. cm.

Includes index.

ISBN 978-1-933176-42-0

1. Cookies. I. Title.

TX772.C6592348 2012

641.86'54--dc23

2011040180

DEDICATION

With love and appreciation: to my mom, Jean, for endless hours teaching me baking, cooking, sewing, stitching, leatherworking and creating; to my husband, Curt, for countless hours tasting cookies, listening to ideas, washing baking dishes and driving me all over the country.
— Kelly

To my wife, Karen, and daughter, Kristi, for always encouraging me, and to my family and friends who have helped me "see the bigger picture."
— Frank

COOKIES

for
Grown-ups

KELLY COOPER
photos by Frank Anzalone

Red Rock Press

New York, NY

Table of Contents

INTRODUCTION

Cookies for Grown-ups evolved somewhere between working on my "to do" list and yearning for more great times with family and friends, where sitting together and sharing events and hopes enhances our relationships. In these moments, food adds a tangible, sensory experience to feelings of love and rootedness. *Cookies for Grown-ups* celebrates flavor, family and friends as well as the fulfilling, creative endeavor of making a gift with our hands that brings texture and taste to great conversation.

You'll find sophisticated flavors and refreshing drink pairings, including wine and cocktails. These cookies both delight the palate and break out of a literal cookie-cutter approach to a customary sweet, crumbly treat.

We all know what a cookie is, right? Sure, a baked, handheld treat often gobbled up within a bite or two. And typically, it is sweet. But the beginnings of the cookie weren't always so sweet.

Records have shown that in the 25th century B.C., the Egyptians were already eating crackers of a sort, and they may have learned how to make them from the Babylonians. Archeologists tell us that by 1300 B.C., Egyptians used wheat and other grains to bake over three dozen types of breads and cakes. Women did the hard work of grinding the grain between rocks. Dough was made from flour and water — without yeast, so bread did not rise. It was usually cooked as flat loaves, sometimes with honey, milk, eggs, fruit or other seasonings. The unleavened bread the Hebrews quickly baked in the desert, after fleeing slavery, sounds similar to Egyptian flatbread.

Baking was advanced in wealthy Roman households, which, by 300 B.C., may have included a pastry cook. The Romans loved huge banquets. By the beginning of the first century A.D., there

were more than 300 pastry chefs in Rome. Romans baked salty goods we might recognize as pretzels, as well as honey cookies and savory sesame crackers that may have been consumed at any time from morning to midnight.

Long after the festivities of ancient Egypt and Rome had ended, simple flour and water concoctions, sometimes salted, and baked into hard sheets or discs, persisted, eventually becoming the hard-tack ships carried as a food staple on long voyages.

Eighth-century Persians were known for their baking of both savory and sweet flour-based goodies. Travelers in the ancient Arab world often carried a quantity of small crackers or cookies in their packs to sustain them. The baking talents of the Near and Middle East probably entered Europe with the Muslims, who flourished in Spain until the 15th century.

Hardtack and various crackers sailed to the New World. In the 1700s, both England and the Netherlands were noted for their sweet crackers called "biscuits" in England, after a now little-used French word, and called *koekje* by the Dutch, the word that evolved into the American cookie.

While many people still associate cookies with sweetness and a limited repertoire of small, dried fruits and gentler spices, in recent years a few culinary artists have talked about more hors d'oeuvre-like "cocktail cookies." For me, any small, baked, hand-held treat — sweet or savory — that provides a bite of pleasure is a cookie. The best cookies help cement relationships and almost all of them go well with a drink. And I don't just mean milk or tea. The recipes in *Cookies for Grown-ups* have complex or surprising flavor

HIT THE SPOT *has a cheese and mustard-flavored base and goes well with beer.*

combinations that might call for a particular cocktail, wine, beer or hot beverage. I offer pairings for my cookies not to dictate the time of day each ought to be consumed, but to suggest the drink I've found that adds to the amusement, romance, comfort or joy of eating a particular cookie.

On today's tables, foods from around the world are converging and morphing into ever more imaginative versions. Previously unusual or hard-to-find ingredients are now readily available in local markets and online. This availability and affordability of herbs, fruits, nuts and spices generate possibilities for creative expression.

The QR (Quick Response) codes presented with every recipe can be scanned with a smart phone QR Reader. They will link to a URL that contains a photo of the recipe and a list of ingredients for quick access in the market. Cookies with a topping that is more time-consuming to prepare offer a less time-consuming base, and vice versa.

One favor I ask of you — when you bake these cookies, take time to relish the color and aroma of each ingredient. Feel free to use your hands in shaping them. Enjoy the taste of each bite. Consider when you learned to bake, perhaps with your mother or grandmother. Remember those who baked for you and the loved ones you bake for today.

The world is wonderful and a little crazy at times; have fun with these cookies and remember to savor the food and people in our lives.

Kelly Cooper
Kelly@GrownUpCookies.com

DARK DESIRE is a bittersweet chocolate treat that is a delightful match for a glass of Port.

Chapter 1

A Toast to the Good Life

We all enjoy the nuances of taste. My first chapter introduces bold and unexpected cookie flavors to share with family and friends, in hopes of evoking memorable stories and new possibilities for happy times. *Cookies for Grown-ups* revels in the good life, where effort, faith and commitment converge.

SCINTILLATING

Milk chocolate, habanero *pepper and orange*

The creamy milk chocolate, balanced with the sunshine of an orange, is fused with the unmistakable heat of a fresh *habanero*. Sandwiched or frosted, this cookie scintillates the senses and demands multiple bites.

Pairing: Chardonnay

1. In a large bowl, using an electric mixer, cream together butter and sugar until light and fluffy, about 3 minutes. Mix in egg, vanilla and orange juice. Beat until well blended.

2. Whisk together flour, baking powder and salt in a small bowl and add to butter mixture. Beat until just incorporated.

3. Form dough into 2 logs (1 inch in diameter) and wrap in parchment paper. Freeze for 30 minutes or refrigerate for 2 hours.

4. Preheat oven to 350° F. Slice logs into ⅛-inch-thick rounds and place 1 inch apart on a parchment-lined or nonstick baking sheet. Bake for 7-9 minutes or until bottoms are light brown. Let sit for a few minutes and transfer to a cooling rack.

5. Melt chocolate bar in a double boiler (or microwave in a separate bowl, in 30-second intervals, typically 3-4 times), gently and stirring often. When melted, mix in *habanero* pepper, orange zest, butter, confectioners' sugar and orange juice. Stir into a creamy frosting consistency. Sandwich or top cookies with frosting.

Yields about 3 dozen, sandwiched, or 6 dozen, open-faced

INGREDIENTS

½ cup unsalted butter, softened
1 cup sugar
1 large egg
2 teaspoons vanilla extract
2 tablespoons fresh orange juice
2 cups all-purpose flour
½ teaspoon baking powder
½ teaspoon salt

FOR FILLING

1 (4.4-ounce) bar high-quality milk chocolate, broken into pieces
1 fresh *habanero* pepper, seeded and finely chopped
1 tablespoon orange zest
1 tablespoon unsalted butter, softened (2 tablespoons, if you bake all open-face)
1 cup confectioners' sugar (2 cups, open-face), sifted
2-4 tablespoons orange juice (7-8 tablespoons, open-face)

QR Code

Shopping List

INGREDIENTS

¾ cup unsalted butter, softened
⅔ cup sugar
⅔ cup light brown sugar, packed
1 large egg
2 tablespoons agave nectar
4 tablespoons Grand Marnier®
   (or plum juice)
2¾ cups all-purpose flour
1¼ teaspoons ground cardamom
1¼ teaspoons ground cinnamon
½ teaspoon baking powder
½ teaspoon baking soda
½ teaspoon salt
1½ cups plums, pitted and roughly
   chopped (small bite-sized pieces)

SMART COOKIE

For more sweetness; top with a buttercream frosting. Mix together until creamy: 2 tablespoons butter, softened; 2 tablespoons Grand Marnier® (or plum juice); 1½ cups confectioners' sugar, sifted. Lightly frost.

LIVELY

Plum, agave nectar, cardamom, Grand Marnier® and cinnamon

Lively captures the taste buds with an "of course!" moment, as we consider familiar flavors that are perhaps not brought together often enough. This cookie can be enjoyed anywhere a fresh spark is needed, whether on a plate or in conversation. It's somehow obvious with a moment of mystery.

Pairing: Iced Tea

1 Preheat oven to 350° F. In a large bowl, using an electric mixer, cream together butter and sugars until light and fluffy, about 3 minutes. Mix in egg, agave nectar and Grand Marnier®. Beat until well blended.

2 Whisk together flour, cardamom, cinnamon, baking powder, baking soda and salt in a small bowl and add to butter mixture. Beat until just incorporated. Refrigerate for 1 hour.

3 Scoop out 1 teaspoon of dough at a time and press 2-3 plum pieces into the dough (or fold in all of the plums and scoop out dough, distributing plums evenly to each cookie and refrigerate for 1 hour). Round each teaspoon of dough with your hands and place 1½ inches apart on a parchment-lined or nonstick baking sheet.

4 Bake for 10-12 minutes or until bottoms are light brown. Let sit for a few minutes and transfer to a cooling rack.

Yields about 4 dozen

Shopping List

JAMAICAN HEAT

Plantain with chipotle pepper and brown sugar on lime and coconut

Jamaican Heat packs a delightful punch with quick-fried plantains dusted with chipotle pepper and brown sugar. The subtly sweet and spicy combination rests on a coconut-lime base that transports the palate to an island vacation.

Pairing: Your Favorite Rum Drink

1 Preheat oven to 350° F. In a small bowl, stir together the light brown sugar, salt and chipotle pepper. Set aside. Slice the plantains into ¼-inch-thick coins or thinner. Coat both sides of each plantain piece with the sugar mixture. In a skillet, heat the oil over medium heat and quickly fry plantains for 1-2 minutes on each side, until the plantains begin to soften. Remove from pan to cool. Set aside.

2 In a large bowl, using an electric mixer, cream together butter and sugar until light and fluffy, about 3 minutes. Mix in egg, vanilla, lime zest and juice. Beat until well blended.

3 Whisk together flour, baking powder, baking soda, salt and coconut flakes and add to butter mixture. Beat until just incorporated.

4 Scoop or drop dough by 1 rounded tablespoon portions and place 1 inch apart on a parchment-lined or nonstick baking sheet. Bake for 5 minutes.

5 Take cookies out of oven and place one plantain slice on each cookie, press lightly, and continue baking until bottoms are golden, for another 7-8 minutes (12-13 minutes total baking time). Let sit for a few minutes and transfer to a cooling rack.

Yields about 4 dozen

Shopping List

INGREDIENTS

3 tablespoons light brown sugar, packed
½ teaspoon coarse salt
1 teaspoon ground chipotle pepper, or to taste
2-3 ripe plantains, peeled
2-3 tablespoons peanut or canola oil
1 cup unsalted butter, softened
1½ cups sugar
1 large egg
½ teaspoon vanilla extract
1 tablespoon lime zest (can substitute lemon)
3 tablespoons lime juice (can substitute lemon)
2¾ cups all-purpose flour
½ teaspoon baking powder
1 teaspoon baking soda
½ teaspoon salt
1 cup shredded coconut flakes, sweetened or unsweetened

SWEET TAPENADE
Dried fig, caramel, balsamic vinegar and cream

Chewy and moist, *Sweet Tapenade* offers an adult take on the dried fig cookies many of us snacked regularly on in our youth, and some of us still do. A hint of balsamic vinegar rounds out the fig topping which rests on a slightly sweet round.

Pairing: Sauvignon Blanc

INGREDIENTS

⅔ cup unsalted butter, softened
¾ cup sugar
2 large eggs
1 teaspoon high-quality balsamic
   vinegar
2 cups all-purpose flour
1 teaspoon ground cinnamon
½ teaspoon baking powder
¼ teaspoon salt

FOR TOPPING

30 soft caramels
6 tablespoons heavy cream
1 cup dried figs, chopped medium fine
2 teaspoons high-quality balsamic
   vinegar

1 Preheat oven to 350° F. In a large bowl, using an electric mixer, cream together butter and sugar until light and fluffy, about 3 minutes. Beat in eggs, 1 at a time, until blended. Mix in balsamic vinegar.

2 Whisk together flour, cinnamon, baking powder and salt in a small bowl and add to butter mixture. Beat until just incorporated.

3 Scoop or drop dough by 1 teaspoon portions and place 1 inch apart on a parchment-lined or nonstick baking sheet. Bake for 10-12 minutes or until edges are light brown. Let sit for a few minutes and transfer to a cooling rack.

4 For topping, heat caramels and cream in a small saucepan over low heat or microwave in a bowl for 3 (30-second) intervals, stirring until thick and smooth. Stir in chopped figs.

5 Spoon ½ teaspoon of the fig mixture onto each cookie. Place 1 drop of balsamic vinegar onto the topping of each cookie. (Note: I dip my finger into the spoon of vinegar and touch a drop onto the topping.)

Yields about 4 dozen

Shopping List

DELECTABLE

Caramelized pear, crystallized ginger and walnut

Inspired by caramelized pear desserts in upscale restaurants, *Delectable's* Bosc pears with underlying hints of butter and brown sugar fuse with the cookie's shortbread-style base and subtle walnut and crystallized ginger flavors. A tin of these bars makes a wonderful hostess gift or addition to a family picnic. Simply delectable.

Pairing: Coffee or Tea

1 Preheat oven to 375° F. Lightly butter the bottom and sides of a 9-inch-by-13-inch baking dish. Set aside. In a large bowl, using an electric mixer, cream together butter, sugar and ⅓ cup light brown sugar until light and fluffy, about 3 minutes. Mix in vanilla, fresh grated ginger root and crystallized ginger. Blend until just incorporated.

2 Whisk together flour, cinnamon and salt in a small bowl and add to butter mixture. Beat until just blended. Stir in walnuts.

3 Press dough into prepared pan (smaller dishes will create a thicker cobbler dish). Spread pears evenly over the dough in pan. Sprinkle remaining ⅓ cup brown sugar over pears. Drizzle melted butter over the top.

4 Bake for 40 minutes or until knife comes out clean. Let cool for 15 minutes. Cut into squares and serve.

Yields about 2 dozen

INGREDIENTS

¾ cup unsalted butter, softened
⅓ cup sugar
⅔ cup light brown sugar, packed, divided
½ teaspoon vanilla extract
1 teaspoon fresh grated ginger root
2 tablespoons crystallized ginger, chopped medium
2 cups all-purpose flour
1 teaspoon ground cinnamon
¼ teaspoon salt
¾ cup walnuts, finely chopped
3½ cups Bosc pears, slivered
3 tablespoons butter, melted

Shopping List

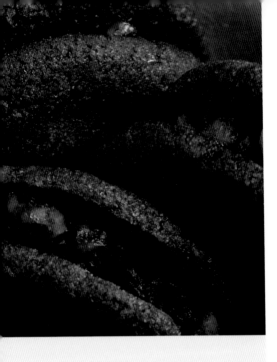

UNEXPECTED

Roasted red pepper, hazelnut, Nutella™ and paprika

Inspired by tapenade, *Unexpected's* roasted peppers, hazelnut and paprika, stirred with Nutella™, create a wonderful bold and sweet explosion. Sandwiched between two cocoa wafers, the ingredients are just as unexpected as their exhilarating result. A great "can I bring something?" surprise to a get-together with friends. Think unexpected tapas dessert.

Pairing: Chocolate Stout

INGREDIENTS

1 dried or fresh ancho chili pepper
or any other medium-intensity
chili pepper
2 red bell peppers
1 cup hazelnuts, raw or roasted,
chopped
1 teaspoon sweet paprika
1 teaspoon hot paprika (can substitute
red chili powder)
¼ cup Nutella™
2 tablespoons red wine vinegar
1 teaspoon olive oil, more if needed
¾ cup unsalted butter, softened
1½ cups sugar
1 large egg yolk
1 teaspoon vanilla extract
1¼ cups all-purpose flour
½ cup unsweetened cocoa powder
½ teaspoon baking soda
½ teaspoon salt

1 Broil and prepare peppers (see SMART COOKIE for detailed instructions). Roughly chop and place in a food processor or blender. Add hazelnuts, paprikas, Nutella™ and vinegar and process until blended well. Slowly add olive oil until mixture reaches a spreadable consistency. Set aside for cookie filling.

2 In a large bowl, using an electric mixer, cream together butter and sugar until light and fluffy, about 3 minutes. Mix in egg yolk and vanilla. Beat until well blended.

3 Whisk together flour, cocoa powder, baking soda and salt in a small bowl and add to butter mixture. Beat until just incorporated.

4 Form dough into 2 logs (1½ inches in diameter) and wrap each in parchment paper. Freeze for 30 minutes or refrigerate for 3 hours.

5 Preheat oven to 350° F. Slice logs into ⅛-inch-thick rounds and place 1 inch apart on a parchment-lined or nonstick baking sheet. Bake for 8-9 minutes or until bottoms begin to brown. Let sit for a few minutes and transfer to a cooling rack.

Shopping List

6 Once cool, top half of the cookies with 1 teaspoon filling and top with another cookie to create a sandwich. If you sandwich all the cookies, there may be ¼ to ½ cup filling remaining; depending on the size of the peppers. Do not overfill; the topping keeps well in the freezer.

Yields about 3 dozen, sandwiched

SMART COOKIE

To broil peppers: Preheat broiler. Line a baking sheet with aluminum foil. Place peppers on pan and broil, turning occasionally, until they are blistered and blackened all around. The more surface blistered and blackened, the better. Place the peppers in a quart-size paper bag (or in a bowl of ice and water) for 15 minutes. When the peppers are cool enough to handle, cut and remove the stems, skins, seeds and membranes.

SATISFACTION

Pear (or peach), blue cheese, lemon and walnut

Satisfaction is a fruit-and-cheese plate all in one cookie. Whether served before or after a meal, this sumptuous soft cookie with a light nut crunch perfectly complements a bubbly wine. If you're making this recipe with a mild blue cheese, use pears. For a strong blue cheese, use peaches.

Pairing: Sparkling Wine

INGREDIENTS

¾ cup unsalted butter, softened

1 cup light brown sugar, packed

1 large egg

1 teaspoon lemon juice

2¼ cups all-purpose flour

¼ teaspoon ground ginger

1½ teaspoons baking soda

¼ teaspoon salt

1 tablespoon fresh ginger root, minced

½ teaspoon fresh thyme, finely chopped

2 Bartlett pears, unpeeled (or 2 peaches, peeled), roughly chopped

¼ teaspoon cracked black pepper

½ cup walnuts, chopped medium

⅓ cup blue cheese crumbles

1 Preheat oven to 350° F. In a large bowl, using an electric mixer, cream together butter and brown sugar until light and fluffy, about 3 minutes. Mix in egg and lemon juice. Beat until well blended.

2 Whisk together flour, ground ginger, baking soda and salt in a small bowl and add to butter mixture. Beat until just incorporated.

3 Stir in fresh ginger, thyme, pears (or peaches), black pepper and walnuts. Do not stir in blue cheese.

4 Scoop or drop dough by 1 teaspoon portions and place 1½ inches apart on a parchment-lined or nonstick baking sheet. Place 1 blue cheese crumble on the center of each cookie. Don't place more than one crumble; more cheese will overwhelm the cookie. Bake for 10-12 minutes or until bottoms are golden brown. Let sit for a couple of minutes and transfer to a cooling rack.

Yields about 4 dozen

Shopping List

PESTO

Walnut, orange zest, Parmesan cheese and fresh basil

Inspired by the sauce from Genoa that may dress pasta or pizza, the cookie I've named *Pesto* is a savory, with walnuts and orange zest adding a twist on tradition. Fresh basil gives a bright finish to this shortbread-like cookie.

Pairing: Pale Lager

INGREDIENTS

½ cup unsalted butter, softened
½ cup sugar
2 large egg yolks
1 tablespoon orange juice
1 tablespoon orange zest
1 tablespoon fresh basil, finely chopped
1½ cups all-purpose flour
½ cup walnuts, finely chopped
½ cup grated Parmesan cheese
Basil leaves for decoration, if desired

1 In a large bowl, using an electric mixer, cream together butter and sugar until light and fluffy, about 3 minutes. Beat in egg yolks until blended. Mix in orange juice, zest and basil.

2 Mix together flour, walnuts and Parmesan in a small bowl and add to butter mixture. Beat until just incorporated.

3 Form dough into a log (2 inches in diameter) and wrap in parchment paper. Press log on counter to form a rectangular shape rather than a round shape. Freeze for 30 minutes or refrigerate for 2 hours.

4 Preheat oven to 375° F. Slice dough into ¼-inch-thick rectangles and place 1 inch apart on a parchment-lined or nonstick baking sheet.

5 Use kitchen scissors or a knife to cut small decorative basil leaf (see photo), press onto each cookie. Bake for 10-12 minutes or until bottoms are light golden brown. Let sit for a few minutes and transfer to a cooling rack.

Yields about 2 dozen

Shopping List

INGREDIENTS

1 red bell pepper
1 large Granny Smith or other green,
   tart apple
⅔ cup grated *Gruyère* cheese
¾ cup unsalted butter, softened
¾ cup sugar
1 large egg
1 teaspoon vanilla extract
2¼ cups all-purpose flour
1 teaspoon baking powder
½ teaspoon salt

— SMART COOKIE

To broil pepper: Preheat broiler. Line a baking sheet with aluminum foil. Place pepper on pan and broil, turning occasionally, until they are blistered and blackened all around. The more surface blistered and blackened, the better. Place the pepper in a quart-size paper bag (or in a bowl of ice and water) for 15 minutes. When the pepper is cool enough to handle, remove the stems, skins, seeds and membranes.

OBSESSION CONFESSION
Roasted red pepper, Granny Smith apple and Gruyère *cheese*

I am obsessed with the combination of roasted pepper and *Gruyère*. I am willing to stand in line for a soup version when it is much too hot outside for a normal person to consume soup. I cruise online for restaurants that may offer the duo in an appetizer or entrée. I have always been a fan of cheese; I am a somewhat recent convert to roasted peppers. I confess that I tested and tasted enough cookies and dough writing this book to negate my obsession. But alas, I bought the soup again when it was over 100 degrees outside.

Pairing: Sparkling Apple Cider

1 Broil and prepare pepper (see SMART COOKIE for detailed instructions). Halve and core the apple. Roughly chop broiled pepper and apple (with skin) and put into a bowl. Sprinkle with grated *Gruyère* and mix.

2 Preheat oven to 375° F. In a large bowl, using an electric mixer, cream together butter and sugar until light and fluffy, about 3 minutes. Mix in egg and vanilla. Beat until well blended.

3 Whisk together flour, baking powder and salt in a small bowl and add to butter mixture. Beat until just incorporated.

4 Shape dough into 1-inch balls then, using your fingers, either press flat or create a thumbprint cookie shape. Spoon 1 teaspoon of the pepper mixture into or on each cookie. Place 1 inch apart on a parchment-lined or nonstick baking sheet. Bake for 10 minutes or until bottoms are golden, then broil on high for an additional 1-2 minutes until cheese begins to bubble and brown. Let sit for a few minutes and transfer to a cooling rack.

Yields about 3 dozen

Shopping List

THE BOLD SISTER
Masa *, chorizo, raisin and pine nut

I wanted to make a cookie with the great corn flavor of the *masa* (the dough) of a tamale. *The Bold Sister* satisfies with a sweet corn texture and a spicy chorizo finished with sweet raisins and soft pine nuts. This savory surprise is a great addition to a casual party or you can bring it to work and have a fiesta.

Pairing: Mexican Pale Lager

1 Soak raisins in hot water until plump, then drain and set aside. In a medium sauté pan over medium-low heat, fry chorizo (no oil needed) until it is cooked and moist, not oily. Stir in raisins and pine nuts until warmed. Set aside.

2 Preheat oven to 375° F. In a large bowl, using an electric mixer, cream together butter and sugar until light and fluffy, about 3 minutes. Mix in egg and vanilla. Beat until well blended.

3 Whisk together flours, baking powder, salt and chili powder in a small bowl and add to butter mixture. Beat until just incorporated. Fold in chorizo mixture.

4 Scoop or drop dough by 1 teaspoon portions and place 1½ inches apart on a parchment-lined or nonstick baking sheet. Bake for 11-13 minutes or until edges begin to brown. Let sit for a few minutes and transfer to a cooling rack.

Yields about 4 dozen

Masa, Spanish for dough, is the often shortened version of *masa de maíz* (corn dough). *Masa* is the dough used in making many Latin American dishes, including tamales.

Shopping List

INGREDIENTS

⅓ cup raisins
½ pound chorizo**
⅓ cup pine nuts
½ cup unsalted butter, softened
1 cup sugar
1 large egg
1 teaspoon vanilla extract
½ cup *masa harina* (corn flour)
1¼ cups all-purpose flour
1 teaspoon baking powder
½ teaspoon salt
½ teaspoon chili powder
  (or cayenne pepper), optional

SMART COOKIE

**Of the many chorizos available, I have tried the more affordable tube, the meat-counter bulk and the specialty-store organic varieties. All work well. The trick is to cook the sausage so the oil reduces, while not drying out the meat.*

TEXTURE

Eggplant, ricotta cheese, Parmesan cheese and walnut

Whenever I eat eggplant, I anticipate its soft and supple texture. This cookie begins with a firm, slightly crisp savory base. Atop are thin slices of sautéed eggplant, followed by a small, sautéed round of cheese and walnut. This wonderful, multilevel bite – perfect for cocktail hour – bursts with flavor.

Pairing: Merlot

INGREDIENTS

1 eggplant, any variety*
1 cup, plus 2 tablespoons, unsalted
   butter, softened, divided
¾ cup sugar
1 large egg
1½ teaspoons vanilla extract
2¾ cups all-purpose flour
¼ teaspoon baking soda
½ teaspoon salt
2 tablespoons olive oil
1½ cups ricotta cheese
1 cup grated Parmesan cheese
½ cup walnuts, chopped medium

SMART COOKIE

Any variety of eggplant can be used. If you use an eggplant small in diameter, such as a Japanese eggplant, you'll need to adjust the way you cut it into pie-slice wedges. For the whole recipe, you will need 100 (⅛-inch-thick) wedges, measuring 1 inch wide at the outer edge. Two wedges for each cookie.

1 Peel eggplant leaving stripes of skin for color (leave half of the skin intact). Slice into ⅛-inch-thick rounds and cut rounds into pie-slice wedges. The curved outer edge of each wedge should measure 1 inch, as should the length from the tip to outer edge. (Two of these small pieces will be placed on each cookie. See photo.) Set aside the eggplant.

2 In a large bowl, using an electric mixer, cream together 1 cup butter and sugar until light and fluffy, about 3 minutes. Mix in egg and vanilla. Beat until well blended.

3 Whisk together flour, baking soda and salt in a small bowl and add to butter mixture. Beat until just incorporated.

4 Form dough into 2 logs (1½ inches in diameter) and wrap each in parchment paper. Freeze for 30 minutes or refrigerate for 2 hours.

5 Heat oil and remaining 2 tablespoons butter in a skillet over medium heat. Quick-fry eggplant for 3 minutes, gently turning and stirring until soft. (The eggplant will warm again when baking, but not cook further.) Remove from skillet, pat dry and set aside. Keep pan for later use, without cleaning.

Shopping List

6 In a small bowl, mix together ricotta cheese, Parmesan and walnuts. Scoop 1½ teaspoons of mixture and form patty, approximately 1 inch wide and ¼ inch-thick. Repeat until the remaining mixture is used up. There will be about 48 patties in all.

7 Put back skillet over medium heat and, using oil in pan, quick-fry the cheese patties over medium heat for 1 minute on each side, to create a crisp, browned outer layer. Some ricotta cheese tends to be watery; if so, the patties may begin to blend. If so, treat as though you are scrambling eggs, continue to stir 2-3 minutes until a light browning and crusting occurs. Set pan of cheese aside.

8 Preheat oven to 375° F. Slice logs into ⅛- to ¼-inch-thick rounds and place 1½ inches apart on a parchment-lined or nonstick baking sheet. Fan 2 eggplant wedges on each cookie, followed by a cheese patty (or slightly under 1 teaspoon of cheese mixture). Press lightly to set eggplant and cheese mixture onto each cookie. Bake for 10-12 minutes or until bottoms are light brown. Let sit for a few minutes and transfer to a cooling rack.

Yields about 4 dozen

INGREDIENTS

1 cup cornmeal

½ cup all-purpose flour

1 teaspoon sugar

1 teaspoon baking powder

1 teaspoon coarse salt

½ teaspoon cracked black pepper

½ teaspoon Italian seasoning*

½ cup grated sharp Cheddar cheese

½ cup grated Provolone cheese

2 tablespoons butter, melted

¼ cup olive oil

1 large egg, stirred

1 tablespoon water

⅓ cup salami, roughly chopped

¼ cup kalamata olives, roughly chopped

¼ cup peperoncini, roughly chopped

── SMART COOKIE ──

Italian seasoning can be purchased pre-packaged or made with any combination of equal parts of any three of: oregano, basil, thyme, rosemary or marjoram.

ANTIPASTO

Cheddar and Provolone cheeses, kalamata olive, peperoncini, salami and Italian seasoning

Antipastos are a little different in every restaurant. This savory cookie version is based on cheese while the kalamata olives, peperoncini and salami add punch and texture. A touch of Italian herbs is a nice finishing note in the light crunch of the cornmeal base. It's amazing how quickly these cookies disappear.

Pairing: American Light Beer

1 Preheat oven to 400° F. In a large bowl, whisk together cornmeal, flour, sugar, baking powder, salt, black pepper and Italian seasoning.

2 Mix in cheeses, butter, olive oil, egg and water until just combined. Then fold in salami, olives and peperoncini.

3 Using your hands so the dough will be dense, scoop out dough by 1 rounded teaspoon portions and place 1 inch apart on a parchment-lined or nonstick baking sheet. Bake for 11-12 minutes or until bottoms are golden. Let sit for a few minutes and transfer to a cooling rack.

Yields about 3 dozen

REDOLENT

Garlic, roasted red pepper and Marcona almond

There's no mistaking garlic, roasted red pepper or almond. They stand bravely in every dish; they assume their places and defy anyone who snubs their positions. *Redolent* knows the character of these talented and demanding actors, and directs this cookie so that each flavor communicates flair, individuality and a resounding performance. If foods could ever be considered character actors, garlic and red pepper would assume their nominations and almond would remind us that a character actor both enhances and intensifies the production.

Pairing: Cosmopolitan

1 In a medium pan, on low heat, sauté 1 tablespoon butter and garlic for 1 minute. Remove from heat as garlic begins to brown. Set aside.

2 In a large bowl, using an electric mixer, cream together remaining 1 cup butter and sugar until light and fluffy, about 3 minutes. Mix in vanilla.

3 Whisk together flour and salt in a small bowl and add to butter mixture. Beat until just incorporated. Stir in chopped almonds. Refrigerate dough for 1 hour.

4 Preheat oven to 325° F. Scoop out dough by 1 teaspoon portions, form balls and then flatten to ¼-inch-thick and place 1½ inches apart on a parchment-lined or nonstick baking sheet. Decorate the top of each cookie with an almond, a piece of red pepper and a piece of cilantro or parsley. Bake for 18-20 minutes or until bottoms are light golden brown. Let sit for a few minutes and transfer to a cooling rack.

Yields about 3 dozen

INGREDIENTS

1 cup, plus 1 tablespoon, unsalted
    butter, softened, divided
1 clove garlic, minced
¼ cup sugar
1 teaspoon vanilla extract
2 cups all-purpose flour
½ teaspoon salt
1½ cups Marcona almonds,
    finely chopped
36 Marcona almonds
36 small pieces marinated roasted
    red peppers
36 small pieces fresh cilantro or parsley

Shopping List

Regardless of the weather, some flavors encourage our taste buds to remember and savor traditions. This chapter invites you to take off your coat and stay awhile. Visit with friends or curl up with a good book. Put your feet up; no one's counting cookies. The cold you want to escape may reflect the temperature or someone's attitude. Either way, come on in and enjoy some warm cookies.

AMERICANA

Sweet potato, maple syrup, cranberry and pecan

Want to take a holiday road trip? *Americana* is a traveling tradition. I decided to go with sweet potato and the tastes that our tongues expect: maple syrup and cranberry. Adding turkey and stuffing seemed a bit much. *Americana* makes a great pre-holiday cookie, 364 days a year.

Pairing: Gewürztraminer

1 Preheat oven to 350° F. In a large bowl, using an electric mixer, cream together butter and sugars until light and fluffy, about 3 minutes. Mix in egg, maple syrup and sweet potato. Beat until well blended.

2 Whisk together flour, oats, ginger, cinnamon, cloves, nutmeg, baking powder, baking soda and salt in a small bowl and add to butter mixture. Beat until just incorporated. Stir in pecans and cranberries. (*If your dried cranberries are soft, add as is. If they seem dry, like a dry raisin, place them in a bowl with ½ cup water, microwave for 1 minute, and drain on paper towel. They will plump and, as a result, not pull moisture from the cookie.)

3 Scoop or drop dough by 1 tablespoon portions and place 1½ inches apart on a parchment-lined or nonstick baking sheet. Bake for 13-15 minutes or until edges are golden. Let sit for a few minutes and transfer to a cooling rack.

Yields about 5 dozen

Shopping List

INGREDIENTS

1 cup unsalted butter, softened
½ cup sugar
½ cup light brown sugar, packed
1 large egg
¼ cup pure maple syrup
1 cup baked sweet potato, cubed
   or mashed
1½ cups all-purpose flour
1½ cups old-fashioned oats
1 teaspoon ground ginger
1 teaspoon ground cinnamon
¼ teaspoon ground cloves
½ teaspoon ground nutmeg
1 teaspoon baking powder
½ teaspoon baking soda
½ teaspoon salt
½ cup pecans, chopped medium
1 cup dried cranberries*

SMART COOKIE

Get prepared: Bake 1 medium to large sweet potato wrapped in aluminum foil at 400° F for 1 hour. Cool, and peel. Now you're ready to mash or cube. You can also substitute the sweet potato with canned yams, which produce a different, but still tasty cookie.

ACQUAINTED
Coconut, dark chocolate and almond

I never tire of the combination of coconut, chocolate and almond. I wanted to create a cookie that showcases each, yet is more about flavor and substance than its candy cousin. *Acquainted* offers bites of familiar flavor with an adult interpretation — moist inside, with an outer crunch; chewy and a little sweet.

Pairing: Cabernet Sauvignon

INGREDIENTS

¾ cup unsalted butter, softened
½ cup light brown sugar, packed
1 teaspoon vanilla extract
½ teaspoon almond extract
1¼ cups all-purpose flour
¼ teaspoon salt
1 cup almonds, finely chopped
1 cup shredded coconut, unsweetened
½ cup mini chocolate chips (for a more
   savory cookie, use cacao nibs)

1 Preheat oven to 350° F. In a large bowl, using an electric mixer, cream together butter and sugar until light and fluffy, about 3 minutes. Mix in vanilla and almond extracts. Beat until well blended.

2 Whisk together flour and salt in a small bowl and add to butter mixture. Beat until just incorporated. Stir in almonds, coconut and chocolate chips.

3 Scoop or drop by 1 rounded teaspoon portions and roll into oval shape in hands. Place each 1 inch apart on a parchment-lined or nonstick baking sheet. Bake for 10-12 minutes or until bottoms are golden brown. Let sit for a few minutes and transfer to a cooling rack.

Yields about 4 dozen

Shopping List

AUNT CAROL
Zucchini, date and walnut

My aunt Carol is in her 80s and lives in a small town in southwestern Oregon. She likes to say that in late summer and early fall, everyone in her town of Cave Junction must remember to lock their doors day and night. It's then the neighbors will try to break in and leave their extra zucchini. In honor of Carol's garden and humor, this rustic cookie offers a wonderful combination of flavor and a touch of home.

Pairing: Hot Apple Cider

1 Preheat oven to 350° F. In a medium sauté pan over low heat, melt 2 tablespoons butter and stir in ¼ cup brown sugar. Add zucchini, dates and walnuts, and increase heat to medium. Stir occasionally for 4-5 minutes or until caramelized. Set aside.

2 In a large bowl, using an electric mixer, cream together remaining butter and 2 cups brown sugar until light and fluffy, about 3 minutes. Beat in eggs, 1 at a time, until blended. Mix in vanilla.

3 Whisk together flour, baking powder, baking soda and salt in a small bowl and add to butter mixture. Beat until just incorporated.

4 Scoop or drop dough by 1 teaspoon portions and place into a very lightly buttered 24-cup mini-muffin pan. Press dough so it covers the bottom and half of the sides, with a recessed center. Do not bring the dough up the full height of the sides. Drop 1-1½ teaspoons of the caramelized mixture into each recessed center. Bake for 9-11 minutes or until edges are golden. Let sit for 15 minutes to cool and gently remove using a knife inserted lightly along the outside edge of each cookie. Transfer to a cooling rack. Repeat with remaining dough and filling.

Yields about 4 dozen

INGREDIENTS

1 cup, plus 2 tablespoons, unsalted butter, softened, divided
2¼ cups light brown sugar, packed, divided
1 cup zucchini, chopped medium
½ cup dried dates, chopped medium
½ cup walnuts, chopped medium
2 large eggs
1½ teaspoons vanilla extract
2¾ cups all-purpose flour
1 teaspoon baking powder
½ teaspoon baking soda
½ teaspoon salt

Shopping List

FAMILIAR MEMORY
Banana, brown sugar, lemon and pecan

I found the original version of this soft, sweet cookie in my grandma's files. The moment I saw her handwriting on the index card, I decided to make something comforting and reminiscent. A quick-fried banana is sandwiched between a butter-crisped bottom and a top layer that gently covers the banana. The single pecan piece atop offers a satisfying crunch. Biting into *Familiar Memory* is like getting a nice hug from home.

Pairing: Milk or English Breakfast Tea

INGREDIENTS

1 cup unsalted butter, plus 4
    tablespoons, softened, divided
1 cup sugar
1 large egg
1 teaspoon vanilla extract
1½ teaspoons lemon zest
2 tablespoons lemon juice
2½ cups all-purpose flour
½ teaspoon baking soda
1 teaspoon salt
4 bananas
6 tablespoons light brown sugar,
    packed
½ cup pecan quarters

1. In a large bowl, using an electric mixer, cream together 1 cup butter and sugar until light and fluffy, about 3 minutes. Mix in egg, vanilla, lemon zest and juice. Blend until well blended.

2. Whisk together flour, baking soda and salt in a small bowl and add to butter mixture. Beat until just incorporated.

3. Form dough into 4 logs (¾ inch in diameter) and wrap each in parchment paper. Freeze for 30 minutes or refrigerate for 1½ hours.

4. While the dough chills, peel and slice 1 banana for each log crossways into ¼-inch-thick slices. For each banana, place 1½ tablespoons light brown sugar on a small plate. Lightly press banana slices in brown sugar, so there is a light amount of sugar on each side. For each banana, melt 1 tablespoon butter in a medium pan over low heat. Quick-fry banana slices for 30 seconds on each side. Remove bananas from the pan, place on a plate and set aside. When all bananas are quick-fried, drizzle the caramelized butter-sugar mixture left in the pan over the top. The bananas don't need to be dried or cooled to proceed.

Shopping List

5 Preheat oven to 400° F. Slice logs in ⅛-inch-thick rounds. Place half of the slices 1½ inches apart on a parchment-lined or nonstick baking sheet. Place 1 banana slice on each cookie. Then top each with 1 remaining dough slice, sandwiching the banana between the two slices. Do not press the dough over the banana. During baking, the top slice will drape over banana to just meet with the bottom. Place 1 pecan quarter on each cookie top, piercing the top slice rather than just laying the pecan on top. Bake for 7-10 minutes or until bottoms are golden brown. The bottom will be lightly crisp, while the top will be soft. Let sit for a few minutes and transfer to a cooling rack. Let set at least 5 minutes before eating.

Yields about 4 dozen

REMEMBERING
Ginger, molasses and spice

This simple ginger cookie satisfies solo, topped with a slice of Brie or sandwiched with vanilla ice cream. It's soft enough to blend nicely in the mouth, but crisp enough on the edges and bottom to really taste the baked ginger and cinnamon-sugar glaze. Its flavor evokes memories of past ginger tastes; *Remembering* is delicious.

Pairing: Riesling

INGREDIENTS

¾ cup unsalted butter, softened
1 cup light brown sugar, packed
1 large egg
⅓ cup molasses
2¼ cups all-purpose flour
2 teaspoons baking soda
1 teaspoon ground ginger
1 teaspoon ground cinnamon
¼ teaspoon ground nutmeg
½ teaspoon salt

FOR GLAZE

3 tablespoons sugar
1 teaspoon ground cinnamon
Small amount of water

1 In a large bowl, using an electric mixer, cream together butter and sugar until light and fluffy, about 3 minutes. Mix in egg and molasses. Beat until well blended.

2 Whisk together flour, baking soda, ginger, cinnamon, nutmeg and salt in a small bowl and add to butter mixture. Beat until just incorporated. Refrigerate 1 hour.

3 Preheat oven to 375° F. Scoop or drop by 1 teaspoon size balls, roll in your hand until smooth, and place 1½ inches apart on a parchment-lined or nonstick baking sheet. Flatten balls slightly with fingers.

4 To make the glaze, stir sugar and cinnamon together in a small bowl. Add a small amount of water — start with 1 teaspoon — to create a thick glaze. Brush a light coating of glaze onto the top of each cookie. Bake for 10-12 minutes. Watch edges as they begin to crisp; take out of the oven before you see a darkened sugar burn. The center will be chewy. Let sit for a few minutes and transfer to a cooling rack.

Yields about 4 dozen

BACK WHEN
Cherry and walnut

Back when I was a kid, cherries were a delicacy. Cherries meant the Fourth of July, summer fruit stands and pie. Walnuts were cracked open for special desserts. *Back When* remembers cherries and walnuts in large, full bites of summer. Just so you know, I might hold the record for fresh cherry consumption.

Pairing: Pinot Noir

1 Preheat oven to 350° F. In a large bowl, using an electric mixer, cream together butter and sugars until light and fluffy, about 3 minutes. Mix in egg and vanilla. Blend until well blended.

2 Whisk together flour, cinnamon, baking soda and salt in a small bowl and add to butter mixture. Beat until just incorporated. Stir in cherries and walnuts.

3 Scoop or drop dough by 1 teaspoon portions and place 1½ inches apart on a parchment-lined or nonstick baking sheet. Bake for 10-12 minutes or until bottoms are golden brown. Let sit for a few minutes and transfer to a cooling rack.

4 If frosting cookies, mix together confectioners' sugar, milk and vanilla in a medium bowl. Consistency should be between a glaze and a frosting. Lightly frost cookies.

Yields about 3 dozen

Shopping List

INGREDIENTS

½ cup unsalted butter, softened
½ cup light brown sugar, packed
¼ cup sugar
1 large egg
½ teaspoon vanilla extract
1¼ cups all-purpose flour
½ teaspoon ground cinnamon
½ teaspoon baking soda
½ teaspoon salt
1 cup fresh cherries, pitted and roughly chopped
½ cup walnuts, roughly chopped

FOR FROSTING (OPTIONAL)
1 cup confectioners' sugar, sifted
3 tablespoons milk
½ teaspoon vanilla extract

SMART COOKIE
If you can't find fresh cherries, fresh blueberries and pecans can be substituted for the cherries and walnuts.

INGREDIENTS

½ cup unsalted butter, softened
½ cup light brown sugar, packed
1 large egg
1 teaspoon vanilla extract
1 cup all-purpose flour
½ teaspoon baking soda
½ teaspoon salt
½ cup hazelnuts, finely chopped
Nutella™ (optional, but obsessively
  recommended)

SMART COOKIE

You can also serve this tasty cookie plain or as a foundation for vanilla ice cream with caramel or chocolate topping.

OH SNAP
Hazelnut and Nutella™

Is Nutella™ a chocolate spread or a nut spread? Perhaps the best way to decide would be to eat one cookie with hazelnuts in mind, and then another cookie with chocolate in mind. Maybe a third can serve as a tie-breaker. Frank, this book's photographer, created the idea for *Oh Snap*, and the cookie is named for how Frank snaps photos of food and food celebrities. He craved a sandwich cookie, not too sweet, with hazelnuts. Oh, and with plenty of Nutella™ on top or inside.

Pairing: Iced Latte

1 In a large bowl, using an electric mixer, cream together butter and sugar until light and fluffy, about 3 minutes. Mix in egg and vanilla. Beat until well blended.

2 Whisk together flour, baking soda and salt in a small bowl and add to butter mixture. Beat until just incorporated. Stir in hazelnuts.

3 Form dough into 2 logs (1 inch in diameter) and wrap in parchment paper. Roll each log on counter to form a consistent round shape. Freeze for 1 hour or refrigerate for 3 hours.

4 Preheat oven to 350° F. Slice logs in ⅛-inch-thick rounds and place 1½ inches apart on a parchment-lined or nonstick baking sheet. Bake for 7-8 minutes or until edges begin to brown. Let sit for a few minutes and transfer to a cooling rack. Sandwich cookies with Nutella™.

Yields about 5 dozen, sandwiched

Shopping List

AUTUMN
Pumpkin, pumpkin seed (pepita), *spice and cream cheese*

After the summer heat but before the holidays, fall baking and cooking produce aromas to entice you back inside. In *Autumn*, pumpkin and its crunchy seeds are coupled with your choice of one of three spice combinations, respectively designed to evoke flavors of a traditional American Thanksgiving dinner, an Indian curry or Mexican empanada. All three speak of autumn, family, sharing and thanks.

Pairing: Pinot Noir

INGREDIENTS

1 cup unsalted butter, softened
½ cup sugar
½ cup light brown sugar, packed
1 large egg
1 teaspoon vanilla extract
1 cup cooked pumpkin, pureéd
2 cups all-purpose flour
1 cup pumpkin seeds (unsalted or
    lightly salted, roasted or raw),
    whole
1 teaspoon baking powder
½ teaspoon baking soda
¼ teaspoon salt

*See facing page for spice combinations,
frosting and decoration.*

1 Preheat oven to 350° F. In a large bowl, using an electric mixer, cream together butter and sugars until light and fluffy, about 3 minutes. Mix in egg, vanilla and pumpkin pureé. Beat until well blended.

2 Whisk together flour, pumpkin seeds, baking powder, baking soda, salt and one of the spice combinations in a small bowl and add to butter mixture. Beat until just incorporated.

3 Scoop or drop dough by 1 teaspoon portions and place 1 inch apart on a parchment-lined or nonstick baking sheet. Bake for 12-13 minutes or until bottoms are golden brown. Let sit for a few minutes and transfer to a cooling rack.

4 To make frosting: In a separate bowl, mix together cream cheese and butter, then add confectioners' sugar, vanilla and milk or cream and mix to a creamy frosting consistency, adding a touch more milk as needed. Frost cookies. Decorate the tops of the cookies with a flower of pumpkin seeds and, if desired, sprinkle with curry powder or cinnamon.

Yields about 4 dozen

Shopping List

SPICE COMBINATIONS

A. Traditional American Thanksgiving
1 teaspoon ground cinnamon
½ teaspoon ground ginger
½ teaspoon ground nutmeg

B. Indian curry
½ teaspoon curry powder
½ teaspoon ground ginger
¼ teaspoon ground coriander
¾ teaspoon ground cumin

C. Mexican empanada
¼ teaspoon ground ginger
⅛ teaspoon ground cloves
½ teaspoon ground cinnamon

FOR FROSTING
AND DECORATION

4 ounces cream cheese, softened
2 tablespoons unsalted
   butter, softened
1 cup confectioners' sugar, sifted
½ teaspoon vanilla extract
1 teaspoon milk or heavy cream
¼ cup pumpkin seeds, whole

Regardless of season, team, athlete or tournament, when it's game time, it is food time. This chapter encourages all sports fans to explore new flavor combinations and a few wild, edible ideas. The name of this eating game is "Fun" while watching your team from a stadium seat or an easy chair in your den. I've also included a cookie to munch while you're driving to the game or taking a hike.

CRUNCH
Pistachios, cacao nibs and crystallized ginger

I like the sensation of crunching on a cookie. *Crunch* offers a great combination of pistachio meats, cacao nibs and crystallized ginger on a slightly sweet base.

Pairing: Coffee or Tea

1 Preheat oven to 400° F. In a large bowl, using an electric mixer, cream together butter and sugar until light and fluffy, about 3 minutes. Mix in egg, vanilla, lemon zest and juice. Beat until well blended.

2 Whisk together flour, baking soda and salt in a small bowl and add to butter mixture. Beat until just incorporated.

3 Evenly sprinkle pistachios, cacao nibs and chopped ginger over mixture. Fold into dough.

4 Using your hands, scoop dough by 1 tablespoon portions, roll into mini logs and place 1½ inches apart on a parchment-lined or nonstick baking sheet. Place 2-3 tablespoons of flour on a small plate. Lightly flour tines of a fork and flatten cookies to ⅛-inch-thickness. Bake for 10-12 minutes or until bottoms begin to brown. Let sit for a few minutes and transfer to a cooling rack.

Yields about 5 dozen

INGREDIENTS

1 cup unsalted butter, softened
1 cup sugar
1 large egg, slightly beaten
1 teaspoon vanilla extract
2 teaspoons lemon zest
2 tablespoons lemon juice
2½ cups all-purpose flour
½ teaspoon baking soda
1 teaspoon salt
1 cup pistachio meats, roughly chopped
⅓ cup cacao nibs*
3 tablespoons crystallized ginger, finely chopped

SMART COOKIE

Cacao nibs are roasted and husked cocoa beans that have been broken into small bits. They can be ordered online or found in specialty food markets. (Mini semisweet chocolate chips can be substituted.)

Shopping List

BUY-ONE, GET-ONE
Raspberry or blackberry or blueberry

When the markets offer a free box of free berries with the purchase of one at full price, it's a great deal, and the berries are typically a day away from being too ripe. I use one package with a salad or on cottage cheese, and the second goes into cookies. I often freeze this dough without fruit in it, then thaw and mix with the berries and bake. Refreshingly simple.

Pairing: Lemonade

INGREDIENTS

½ cup unsalted butter, softened
¾ cup sugar
1 large egg
2 teaspoons vanilla extract
1½ cups all-purpose flour
½ teaspoon ground cinnamon
1 teaspoon cream of tartar
½ teaspoon baking soda
¼ teaspoon salt
1 cup berries, halved
½ cup almonds, roughly chopped
(optional)

1 Preheat oven to 375° F. In a large bowl, using an electric mixer, cream together butter and sugar until light and fluffy, about 3 minutes. Mix in egg and vanilla. Beat until well blended.

2 Whisk together flour, cinnamon, cream of tartar, baking soda and salt in a small bowl and add to butter mixture. Beat until just incorporated. Fold in berries and, if using, almonds.

3 Scoop or drop dough by 1 teaspoon portions and place 1½ inches apart on a parchment-lined or nonstick baking sheet. Bake for 10-12 minutes or until bottoms begin to brown. Let sit for a few minutes and transfer to a cooling rack.

Yields about 4 dozen

Shopping List

TRIBUTE
Carrot, cream cheese and molasses

My husband Curt likes carrot cake, so I created this treat encapsulating carrot, raisin and cream cheese. It's a bit less sweet than the cake, but still moist and creamy, with a tiny crunch of raw carrot on top.

Pairing: Coffee or Tea

1 In a large bowl, using an electric mixer, cream together butter, ¾ cup sugar and ¼ cup light brown sugar until light and fluffy, about 3 minutes. Mix in egg and ¼ cup molasses. Beat until well blended.

2 Whisk together flour, cinnamon, ginger, cloves, baking soda and salt in a small bowl and add to butter mixture. Beat until just incorporated. Refrigerate for 30 minutes.

3 Preheat oven to 350° F. In a medium pan, heat olive oil on medium heat and add chopped carrots. After the carrots have cooked for 4 minutes, turn off the flame and stir in remaining 4 teaspoons molasses and ¼ cup light brown sugar. Set aside.

4 Scoop or drop 1 teaspoon dough into a nonstick or lightly buttered 24-cup mini-muffin pan. Flatten the dough into the bottom of each mini-muffin, don't line the sides with the dough. Place 1 teaspoon carrot mixture onto each cookie. Bake for 15 minutes. The cookies will indent on the top when they bake. Let sit for 15 minutes and pop out of the mini-muffin pan with a spoon. Transfer to a cooling rack. Repeat until all dough and filling are used.

5 To make frosting: Mix together cream cheese, butter, confectioners' sugar and vanilla. Frost each cookie, and top each cookie with a few pieces of carrot for decoration. Refrigerate extra cookies.

Shopping List

Yields about 4 dozen

INGREDIENTS

¾ cup unsalted butter, softened
¾ cup sugar
½ cup light brown sugar, packed, divided
1 large egg
¼ cup molasses, plus 4 teaspoons, molasses, divided
2 cups all-purpose flour
1 teaspoon ground cinnamon
½ teaspoon ground ginger
¼ teaspoon ground cloves
2 teaspoons baking soda
½ teaspoon salt
2 tablespoons olive oil
3 cups carrots, peeled and finely chopped

FOR FROSTING
6 ounces cream cheese, softened
¼ cup unsalted butter, softened
¾ cup confectioners' sugar, sifted
½ teaspoon vanilla extract
¼ cup carrots, peeled and finely chopped

COOKIE BOMB

Jägermeister™, Red Bull™ and dried cherry

There's no reason why champion-season cookies can't be cool, in-your-face, party material like cocktails. *Cookie Bomb* drops an exciting combination of tart fruit and smooth herbal liqueur as it entertains the taste buds. Mixologists have nothing on bakers.

Pairing: Light Beer

INGREDIENTS

¾ cup unsalted butter, softened
½ cup sugar
½ cup light brown sugar, packed
1 large egg
3 tablespoons Jägermeister™
¼ cup Red Bull™
1 cup dried cherries, roughly
    chopped
3 cups all-purpose flour
½ teaspoon baking powder
½ teaspoon baking soda
½ teaspoon salt

FOR FROSTING

2 tablespoons butter, softened
2 tablespoons Jägermeister™
2 tablespoons Red Bull™
2 cups confectioners' sugar, sifted

1   Preheat oven to 350° F. In a large bowl, using an electric mixer, cream together butter and sugars until light and fluffy, about 3 minutes. Mix in egg, Jägermeister™ and Red Bull™. Beat until well blended. Stir in chopped cherries.

2   Whisk together flour, baking powder, baking soda and salt in a small bowl and add to butter mixture. Beat until just incorporated.

3   Scoop or drop dough by 1 rounded teaspoon portions and place 1 inch apart on a parchment-lined or nonstick baking sheet. Bake for 9-10 minutes or until bottoms are golden. Let sit for a few minutes and transfer to a cooling rack.

4   To make frosting: In a separate bowl, mix together butter, Jägermeister™ and Red Bull™. Add confectioners' sugar and mix to a desired frosting consistency. Frost cooled cookies.

Yields about 4 dozen

Shopping List

TRAIL MIX

Trail mix, your favorite variety

I like to eat trail mix while driving and hiking, but pieces always drop in my lap or on the ground. So I created a cookie that makes it possible to eat it with one hand on the steering wheel or while carrying a refillable water bottle. Baking the dough in a biscotti style results in a nice crisp cookie, although not as hard as a true biscotti. You can use your choice of trail mix for this recipe — my favorite has large pieces of almonds. Regardless, this light cookie satisfies when you're on the go.

Pairing: Water

1 In a large bowl, using an electric mixer, cream together butter and sugar until light and fluffy, about 3 minutes. Beat in eggs, 1 at a time, until blended. Mix in vanilla.

2 Whisk together flour, baking powder and salt in a small bowl and add to butter mixture. Beat until just incorporated. Stir in trail mix. Refrigerate dough for 30 minutes.

3 Preheat oven to 350° F. Shape dough into a 10-by-3-by-¾-inch loaf and place on a parchment-lined or nonstick baking sheet. Bake for 30-35 minutes, until the loaf begins to turn golden. Cool for 30 minutes.

4 Lower oven temperature to 325° F. Using a large, sharp knife (to cleanly cut through nuts), slice into ½-inch sections. (Slice at a diagonal, if you want a more biscotti-like appearance.) Lay each piece on its side on baking sheet. Bake for 15-20 minutes or until golden.

Yields about 1½ dozen

INGREDIENTS

½ cup unsalted butter, softened
¾ cup light brown sugar, packed
2 large eggs
1 teaspoon vanilla extract
2¼ cups all-purpose flour
½ teaspoon baking powder
¼ teaspoon salt
2½ cups trail mix, your favorite variety

Shopping List

CURVEBALL
Sweet onion, orange and poppy seed

My Grandpa John was an onion man. He enjoyed white bread sandwiches with a thick slice of sweet onion and an occasional swipe of mayonnaise. Even more than an onion man, he was a baseball man — well, a Dodgers fan. *Curveball* pitches sweet onion as a baked flavor that spans sweet and savory. *Curveball* is best eaten as a snack while you take an afternoon to watch your favorite baseball team.

Pairing: Sparkling Water

INGREDIENTS

1 cup unsalted butter, softened
½ cup confectioners' sugar, sifted
1½ teaspoons poppy seeds
1 teaspoon orange juice
1 tablespoon orange zest
2¼ cups all-purpose flour
¼ teaspoon salt
1 cup sweet onion, such as Vidalia,
    finely chopped

1 In a large bowl, using an electric mixer, cream together butter and sugar until light and fluffy, about 3 minutes. Mix in poppy seeds, orange juice and zest. Beat until well blended.

2 Whisk together flour and salt in a small bowl and add to butter mixture. Beat until just incorporated. Fold in chopped onions. Refrigerate dough for 1 hour.

3 Preheat oven to 325° F. Scoop or drop dough by 1 teaspoon portions and place 1 inch apart on a parchment-lined or nonstick baking sheet. Bake for 20 minutes or until bottoms are golden brown. Let sit for a few minutes and transfer to a cooling rack.

Yields about 4 dozen

Shopping List

REFRESCANTE

Cornmeal, Parmesan cheese, cream cheese and jalapeno pepper

Inspired by a Mexican *sopa*, a cornmeal shallow bowl filled with delicious cheese, sour cream, tomato, pepper and optional meats, *Refrescante's* base is a flaky sweet-corn crunch. Filled with Parmesan, cream cheese, lemon and jalapeno, the cookie's creamy, spicy center creates a wonderful hot-cool sensation. Out of the hundreds of cookies my husband agreeably tasted as I wrote this book, this stands out as his favorite.

Pairing: Margarita

1 Preheat oven to 350° F. In a large bowl, using an electric mixer, cream together butter and sugar until light and fluffy, about 3 minutes. Mix in lemon zest, 1 teaspoon lemon juice and egg yolks. Beat until well blended.

2 Whisk together flour, cornmeal and salt in a small bowl and add to butter mixture. Beat until just incorporated.

3 Shape dough into 1-inch diameter balls and, using your thumb, press a deep well into each. Place 1 inch apart on a parchment-lined or nonstick baking sheet. Bake for 12 minutes or until bottoms are golden. Let sit for a few minutes and transfer to a cooling rack.

4 In a separate bowl, mix cheeses, remaining 3 teaspoons lemon juice, and ¼ cup jalapeno until smooth. Adjust consistency with lemon juice so it is soft enough to not crack the cookie when filling. Fill cooled cookies. Using the remaining 2 tablespoons chopped jalapenos, top each with a small piece of pepper. Keep refrigerated in an airtight container until serving. Best served the day of assembly.

Yields about 2 dozen

INGREDIENTS

¾ cup unsalted butter, softened

⅓ cup sugar

2 teaspoons lemon zest

4 teaspoons lemon juice, divided

3 large egg yolks

2 cups all-purpose flour

½ cup cornmeal

½ teaspoon coarse salt

¾ cup shredded Parmesan cheese

¾ cup cream cheese, at room temperature

¼ cup, plus 2 tablespoons, fresh or canned jalapeno pepper, finely chopped (with juice if canned), divided

Shopping List

INGREDIENTS

½ cup unsalted butter, softened

1 cup sugar

1 large egg

1½ teaspoons lemon juice

1 tablespoon lemon zest

2 cups all-purpose flour

½ teaspoon baking powder

½ teaspoon salt

FOR VEGETABLE PREPARATION AND ASSEMBLY

2 tablespoons olive oil

6 spears asparagus, cut equally into 24 pieces

2-3 young zucchini, cut equally into 24 slices

3 yellow squash, cut equally into 24 slices

24 whole cherry tomatoes

2 tablespoons balsamic vinegar

48 (½-inch-square) slices Asiago cheese (or any semi-hard cheese)

Special equipment: 2 dozen (6-inch) wooden skewers

SAVORY KEBAB

Zucchini, yellow squash, tomatoes, asparagus and Asiago cheese

Distinctive flavors of vegetables and cheese, along with the crunch of a cookie, create this pleasing combination of texture and taste. I love to cook with vegetables. Their savory and sweet flavors and their various textures make veggies wonderful cookie ingredients. Serve these kebabs on a platter for entertaining or as a satisfying, small-plate meal.

Pairing: Chardonnay

1 In a large bowl, using an electric mixer, cream together butter and sugar until light and fluffy, about 3 minutes. Mix in egg, lemon juice and zest. Beat until well blended.

2 Whisk together flour, baking powder and salt in a small bowl and add to butter mixture. Beat until just incorporated.

SMART COOKIE

Use your preference of vegetables for these kebabs. You can choose any combination as long as you have about 100 pieces total. When sautéing, take into account those vegetables that need more time, such as asparagus tips or carrots. I often substitute Gruyère or Cheddar cheese.

Shopping List

3 Form dough into 2 logs (2 inches in diameter) and wrap each in parchment paper. Freeze for 30 minutes or refrigerate for 3 hours.

4 Preheat oven to 350° F. Slice logs into ¼-inch-thick rounds. You may quarter the rounds or use whole cookies. Place each dough quarter or circle 1 inch apart on a parchment-lined or nonstick baking sheet. Bake for 8-10 minutes or until bottoms are golden brown. Let sit for a few minutes and transfer to a cooling rack.

5 To prepare vegetables: Heat oil, over medium heat, in a large sauté pan or skillet. Sauté vegetables until they begin to soften. Start with the asparagus for 4 minutes, then add in the zucchini and squash for an additional 3 minutes. Add in the tomatoes for 2 more minutes. Add vinegar and continue to cook until it glazes the vegetables, about 2 minutes. Set aside.

6 To assemble kebabs: With the point of each skewer, pierce with a gentle turning of the skewer: 4 small cookies or cookie quarters, 4 vegetable pieces and 2 cheese squares. For each skewer, alternate cookies between each piece of vegetable and cheese. Feel free to experiment with the number and shape of cookie and vegetable pieces.

Yields about 2 dozen kebab skewers

INGREDIENTS

½ cup unsalted butter, softened

½ cup sugar

1 large egg

1 teaspoon vanilla extract

1 cup all-purpose flour

½ cup cornmeal

½ teaspoon baking soda

½ teaspoon coarse salt

½ teaspoon ground white pepper
(optional)

1½ cups Granny Smith or other tart
apples, peeled, cored and grated

1½ cups sharp Cheddar cheese, grated

¼ cup finely chopped jalapeno (or ½
cup for more heat)

1 tablespoon fresh cilantro, chopped
(or 1 teaspoon dried)

SMART COOKIE

*For an alternate version of this cookie,
substitute ½ cup old-fashioned
oats for the cornmeal and use ¼
cup dried cranberries and ¼ cup
chopped walnuts in place of the
jalapeno and cilantro.*

SNACKING

Cheddar cheese, apple, jalapeno pepper and cilantro

Snacking's flavors hit the spot with Cheddar and apple, followed by a kick
of jalapeno. Delicious throughout the day, this savory cookie serves up well
with company at a weekend gathering, and is also great as a grab-and-go
snack for work.

Pairing: Soda

1 Preheat oven to 375° F. In a large bowl, using an electric mixer, cream
together butter and sugar until light and fluffy, about 3 minutes. Mix
in egg and vanilla. Beat until well blended.

2 Whisk together flour, cornmeal, baking soda, salt and pepper in a
small bowl and add to butter mixture. Beat until just incorporated.

3 Stir in grated apple, cheese, jalapeno and cilantro.

4 Scoop or drop dough by 1 teaspoon portions and place 1½ inches
apart on a parchment-lined or nonstick baking sheet. Bake for 15
minutes or until bottoms are golden brown. Let sit for a few minutes and
transfer to a cooling rack.

Yields about 3 dozen

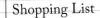

MANCOOKIE

Slim Jim™, beer, dry-roasted sunflower kernels and lime

The *ManCookie* is best served with attitude. No need to explain. Put them on a plate next to a cold drink before a game … and watch them disappear. These are especially recommended for men who think they are more "chips and dip" types than cookie guys. And, for me, there is something surreal in chopping up Slim Jims™ for baking.

Pairing: Beer

1 Preheat oven to 350° F. In a large bowl, using an electric mixer, cream together butter and sugars until light and fluffy, about 3 minutes. Mix in egg, beer and lime zest. Beat until well blended.

2 Whisk together flour, baking powder, baking soda and salt in a small bowl and add to butter mixture. Beat until just incorporated. Fold in Slim Jim™ pieces and sunflower kernels.

3 Scoop or drop dough by 1 rounded tablespoon portions and place 1½ inches apart on a parchment-lined or nonstick baking sheet. Bake for 8-10 minutes or until bottoms are golden. Let sit for a few minutes and transfer to a cooling rack.

Yields about 4 dozen

Shopping List

INGREDIENTS

¾ cup unsalted butter, softened
½ cup sugar
½ cup light brown sugar, packed
1 large egg
¼ cup beer (any brand, more flavorful is better than a light beer)
1 tablespoon lime zest
3 cups all-purpose flour
½ teaspoon baking powder
¼ teaspoon baking soda
½ teaspoon salt
1 cup Slim Jim™, sliced or chopped (about 2 Slim Jim™ sticks)
1¼ cups dry roasted sunflower kernels (non-dry roasted are oily)

Tempting moments.
An intoxicating aroma.
A gentle caress. This
chapter celebrates
special times for two:
rare occasions when
everyone and everything
else fades. These cookies
— particularly when
delectably paired —
seduce taste buds
and enhance intimate
conversations.

INTERLUDE

Fresh mint, white chocolate and cashew

Karen Anzalone, wife of *Cookies for Grown-ups'* photographer, Frank Anzalone, suggested a romantic cookie to eat in an intimate moment. Of course, this cookie is bite-sized — it's much sexier to offer a sweet morsel of white chocolate, cashew and mint before another kiss than to have crumbs on the corner of your mouth.

Pairing: Rosé

1 Preheat oven to 375° F. In a large bowl, using an electric mixer, cream together butter and sugar until light and fluffy, about 3 minutes. Mix in egg, egg yolk and vanilla. Beat until well blended.

2 Whisk together flour, baking soda, baking powder and salt in a small bowl and add to butter mixture. Beat until just incorporated.

3 In a small bowl, mix together mint, cashews and white chocolate. Set aside.

4 Scoop or drop dough by ½ teaspoon portions and place 1 inch apart on a parchment-lined or nonstick baking sheet. Using your finger, make a small indentation in the top of each portion to form a small scoop. Fill each scoop with ¼ teaspoon of the chocolate mixture. Lightly pat the top of the cookie so the filling sets. Bake for 7-9 minutes or until bottoms are just golden. Let sit for a few minutes and transfer to a cooling rack.

Yields about 5 dozen

Shopping List

INGREDIENTS

¾ cup unsalted butter, softened
1¼ cups sugar
1 large egg, plus 1 egg yolk
1½ teaspoons vanilla extract
2 cups all-purpose flour
½ teaspoon baking soda
½ teaspoon baking powder
½ teaspoon salt
2 tablespoons fresh mint, finely chopped
⅓ cup roasted, unsalted cashews, finely chopped
½ cup white chocolate, finely chopped

POPPERS

Raisin, golden raisin and whiskey

These small bites brushed with a rum-laced doughnut glaze bring together fun flavors and a pop-them-in-your-mouth experience. These cookies, dotted with plump raisins simmered in whiskey, are a delicious mix of sweet and strong flavors.

Pairing: Cabernet Sauvignon

INGREDIENTS

⅓ cup, plus 1 tablespoon, whiskey, divided
¾ cup raisins
¾ cup golden raisins
½ cup unsalted butter, softened
¾ cup sugar
1½ teaspoons vanilla extract
1½ cups all-purpose flour
½ teaspoon baking soda
1 teaspoon cream of tartar
¼ teaspoon salt

FOR GLAZE

¼ teaspoon vanilla extract
¼ cup whiskey
¼ teaspoon salt
1½ cups confectioners' sugar, sifted

1 Preheat oven to 375° F. In a small saucepan, over medium-low heat, bring ⅓ cup whiskey and raisins to a boil. Reduce heat and simmer for 10 minutes. Remove from heat and set aside to cool.

2 In a large bowl, using an electric mixer, cream together butter and sugar until light and fluffy, about 3 minutes. Mix in remaining 1 tablespoon whiskey and vanilla. Beat until well blended.

3 Whisk together flour, baking soda, cream of tartar and salt in a small bowl and add to butter mixture. Beat until just incorporated.

4 Drain raisins from cooled whiskey mixture. Stir raisins into dough. Scoop or drop dough by ½ teaspoon portions and place 1 inch apart on a parchment-lined or nonstick baking sheet. Bake for 10-12 minutes or until bottoms are just golden. Let sit for a few minutes and transfer to a cooling rack.

5 To make glaze: In a small bowl, stir together vanilla, whiskey and salt. Mix in confectioners' sugar until you reach a consistency similar to a doughnut glaze. Drizzle glaze over each cookie to coat. Let set.

Yields about 5 dozen

Shopping List

TRYST

Blackberry, yogurt, cinnamon and sugar

The crisp sugar cookie and rich tang of yogurt and blackberries create this *Cookies for Grown-ups* version of chips and dip. The refreshing berry-yogurt dip pops with flavor and color. A small amount of dip keeps the spotlight on the cookie's sweet simplicity. Add a little more dip, and you have a bold fruit experience with a complementary crunch.

Pairing: Green Tea or Merlot

1 In a large bowl, using an electric mixer, cream together butter and 1 cup sugar until light and fluffy, about 3 minutes. Mix in egg and vanilla or mint extract. Beat until well blended.

2 Whisk together flour, baking soda, baking powder and salt in a small bowl and add to butter mixture. Beat until just incorporated.

3 Form dough into 2 logs (2 inches in diameter) and wrap each in parchment paper. Press logs on counter to form a rectangular shape rather than a round shape. Freeze for 30-60 minutes or refrigerate for 2 hours.

4 Preheat oven to 350° F. Slice logs into ¼-inch-thick rectangles. Place raw sugar on a plate; lightly press each slice in sugar, coating both sides. Arrange slices 1 inch apart on a parchment-lined or nonstick baking sheet. Bake for 10-12 minutes or until bottoms begin to brown. Let sit for a few minutes and transfer to a cooling rack.

5 To make dip: In a separate bowl, mix together yogurt, blackberries, honey and cinnamon. (Greek yogurt is thicker in texture. If you substitute with another yogurt, drain and/or add ¼ cup of sour cream.) Serve as a dip with cookies.

Shopping List

Yields about 4 dozen

INGREDIENTS

¾ cup unsalted butter, softened
1 cup sugar
1 large egg
1 teaspoon vanilla or mint extract
2½ cups all-purpose flour
¼ teaspoon baking soda
½ teaspoon baking powder
¼ teaspoon salt
¼ cup raw sugar

FOR DIP
1 cup plain Greek yogurt
2 cups blackberries, quartered
1 tablespoon honey
½ teaspoon ground cinnamon

INVITING

Pineapple, rum, coconut and brown sugar

The sweet, chunky topping offers the favorite tastes of pineapple, coconut and rum in a tapenade style. Served on a deliciously simple cookie; every bite is filled with texture, sweetness and a nod to living on a tropical island.

Pairing: Coffee with a Shot of Rum

INGREDIENTS

½ cup unsalted butter, softened
1 cup sugar
1 large egg
1 teaspoon coconut extract (vanilla extract can substitute)
2 cups all-purpose flour
½ teaspoon baking powder
¼ teaspoon salt

FOR TOPPING

2 tablespoons unsalted butter
½ cup light brown sugar, packed
1½ cups chopped fresh pineapple
⅔ cup shredded coconut
3 tablespoons rum, or to taste

1 In a large bowl, using an electric mixer, cream together butter and sugar until light and fluffy, about 3 minutes. Mix in egg and coconut extract. Beat until well blended.

2 Whisk together flour, baking powder and salt in a small bowl and add to butter mixture. Beat until just incorporated.

3 Form dough into 2 logs (1½ inches in diameter) and wrap each in parchment paper. Roll logs on counter to form a consistent round shape. Freeze for 30 minutes or refrigerate for 2 hours.

4 Preheat oven to 325° F. Slice logs into ¼-inch-thick rounds. Arrange slices 1½ inches apart on a parchment-lined or nonstick baking sheet. Bake for 13-15 minutes or until bottoms are golden brown. Let sit for a few minutes and transfer to a cooling rack.

5 To make topping: In a medium saucepan, sauté butter, brown sugar and pineapple over medium heat. Bring to a low boil. Reduce heat to low. Stir in shredded coconut and rum, simmer for 3 minutes. Place 1 rounded teaspoon of pineapple mixture onto each cookie.

Yields about 3 dozen

Shopping List

CHEERS

Almond, rum, orange and raisin

Cheers to the almond, with its crunch like no other. Here's to the nuance of rum, how it warms us inside. Let us honor the orange, full of refreshing juice. And raise a glass to raisins, those small bites of sweetness. Most of all, cheers to the marriage of ingredients we salute with this cookie!

Pairing: Black Tea or Scotch

1 In a small saucepan, over low heat, bring raisins, ¼ cup rum and ¼ cup orange juice to a simmer. Cook for 15 minutes or until the mixture has cooked down and only 1-2 teaspoons of liquid remains. Set aside.

2 Preheat oven to 350° F. In a large bowl, using an electric mixer, cream together butter and sugars until light and fluffy, about 3 minutes. Mix in remaining 1 tablespoon rum, 2 teaspoons orange juice and zest. Beat until well blended.

3 Whisk together flour, baking soda and salt in a small bowl and add to butter mixture. Beat until just incorporated.

4 Drain raisins and stir into dough, along with the almonds. Scoop or drop dough by 1 rounded teaspoon-portion and place 1½ inches apart on a parchment-lined or nonstick baking sheet. Bake for 12-13 minutes or until bottoms are golden brown. Let sit for a few minutes and transfer to a cooling rack.

Yields about 4 dozen

INGREDIENTS

1 cup raisins
¼ cup, plus 1 tablespoon, rum, divided
¼ cup, plus 2 teaspoons, fresh orange juice, divided
¾ cup unsalted butter, softened
½ cup sugar
½ cup light brown sugar, packed
1 tablespoon orange zest
2 cups all-purpose flour
½ teaspoon baking soda
¼ teaspoon salt
1 cup almonds, chopped medium

Shopping List

INGREDIENTS

2 (4-ounce) high-quality dark or
   bittersweet chocolate bars (70% cacao),
   divided
1 cup unsalted butter, softened
1½ cups light brown sugar, packed
1 large egg
1 teaspoon vanilla extract
2⅓ cups all-purpose flour
½ cup unsweetened cocoa powder
¼ teaspoon baking powder
¼ teaspoon salt
¼ cup fresh thyme, roughly chopped

SMART COOKIE

For an alternate presentation, seen in above photo: Scoop or drop dough by 1 rounded teaspoon portions and roll into smooth balls. Using your finger, create a small indentation into the top of each ball. Place a pinch of thyme and then a square of chocolate into the indentation. Loosely close the cookie around the thyme and chocolate.

DARK DESIRE
Bittersweet chocolate and fresh thyme

A fantasy hidden in a private corner of your mind is where *Dark Desire* originates, a place where the unlikely lovers, dark chocolate and fresh thyme, jubilantly come together. *Dark Desire* is an intimate cookie that pairs well with decadence and secrets.

Pairing: Port

1 Fill the bottom half of a double boiler with water, making certain the top half doesn't touch the water. Bring the water to a simmer. Place 1 (4-ounce) chocolate bar, broken into small pieces, in the top half, and place over the simmering water. Stir frequently until the chocolate is almost melted. Remove from heat and set aside. (To quickly melt chocolate, microwave in a bowl, in 3 to 4 30-second intervals, stirring in between each until smooth.)

2 In a large bowl, using an electric mixer, cream together butter and brown sugar until light and fluffy, about 3 minutes. Mix in egg, vanilla and melted chocolate. Beat until well blended.

3 Whisk together flour, cocoa, baking powder and salt in a small bowl and add to butter mixture. Beat until just incorporated.

4 Form dough into 2 logs (1½ inches in diameter) and wrap each in parchment paper. Roll logs on counter to form a consistent round shape. Freeze for 1 hour or refrigerate for 3 hours.

Shopping List

5 Preheat oven to 350° F. Using remaining chocolate bar, cut or break into ½-inch squares. Set aside. Slice logs into ¼-inch-thick rounds. Place each cookie 1 inch apart on a parchment-lined or nonstick baking sheet. Place a pinch of thyme, followed by a square of chocolate, on the center of each cookie. Bake for 10 minutes or until bottoms are golden brown. Let sit for a few minutes and transfer to a cooling rack.

Yields about 6 dozen

THREE-WAY

Strawberry, Brie cheese, balsamic vinegar, pepper, cucumber and lemon

Inspired by cooking shows where entrées are often prepared in three ways, this cookie features strawberries: with Brie cheese; with cream cheese, cucumber and lemon; with balsamic vinegar and pepper. One dough complements each approach. The trio of variations makes for an attractive presentation on a platter for guests and satisfies a multitude of tastes.

Pairing: Pinot Grigio

1 In a large bowl, using an electric mixer, cream together butter and brown sugar until light and fluffy, about 3 minutes. Mix in egg and lemon zest. Beat until well blended.

2 Whisk together flour, ginger, cream of tartar, baking soda and salt in a small bowl, and add to butter mixture. Beat until just incorporated.

3 Form dough into 2 logs (1½ inches in diameter) and wrap each in parchment paper. Freeze for 30 minutes or refrigerate for 2 hours.

4 Preheat oven to 350° F. Slice logs into ⅛- to ¼-inch-thick rounds. You want each log to yield about 30 cookies. Place each cookie 1 inch apart on a parchment-lined or nonstick baking sheet. Bake for 10 minutes or until bottoms are golden brown. Let sit for a few minutes and transfer to a cooling rack.

INGREDIENTS

½ cup unsalted butter, softened
1 cup light brown sugar, packed
1 large egg
1 tablespoon lemon zest
1½ cups all-purpose flour
¼ teaspoon ground ginger
½ teaspoon cream of tartar
½ teaspoon baking soda
¼ teaspoon salt
1 pint strawberries
3 ounces Brie cheese, softened
2 teaspoons balsamic vinegar
½ teaspoon coarsely-ground black pepper
1 small (or ½ large) cucumber, peeled and chopped
2 ounces cream cheese, softened
1 teaspoon lemon juice

Shopping List

5 Divide the cookie bases into three groups of about the same number; you'll likely have 17-21 cookies in each group. Set the unfinished cookies aside. Then pick out the top (largest, best-looking) ⅔ of your pint of strawberries, and cut them into ⅛- to ¼-inch-thick slices.

a) Take the first group of cookies and top each with Brie — use a small slice or spread 1 teaspoon of the cheese if it's creamy. Take one half of your sliced strawberries and place a strawberry slice on each Brie-topped cookie.

b) Take the second group of cookies and use your remaining berry slices to top each one. Dribble 4-6 drops of balsamic vinegar over each strawberry-topped cookie, plus a small sprinkle of black pepper.

c) To make the topping for the third group of cookies, chop the remaining strawberries (about ⅓ of the original pint). In a bowl, mix the chopped strawberries, the cucumber chopped earlier, the softened cream cheese and lemon juice. Spread onto the cookies.

Yields about 5 dozen

Chapter 5

Ladies Who Lunch

We all have priorities in our lives: family, friends, work. *Cookies for Grown-ups* appreciates the close bonds we form with special women in our lives, whether a relative, a school friend or a colleague. We may see our special girlfriends daily at work or just once a decade. Somehow these friendships remain even as everything around them changes. These recipes celebrate such special connections.

C2

Mascarpone, maple and pistachio

Think of your favorite cream-filled candy. Next, imagine an ambrosial maple cookie, followed by the satisfying crunch of pistachios. Finally, experience *C2* — all three components in every bite. Paired with conversation with friends, *C2* makes for a delicious afternoon.

Pairing: Green Tea or Chenin Blanc

1 Preheat oven to 375° F. In a large bowl, using an electric mixer, cream together butter and sugar until light and fluffy, about 3 minutes. Mix in egg and maple extract. Beat until well blended.

2 Whisk together flour, baking powder and salt in a small bowl and add to butter mixture. Beat until just incorporated.

3 Scoop or drop dough by 1 rounded teaspoon portions into each cup of a nonstick or lightly buttered 24-cup mini-muffin pan. Press dough so it covers the bottom and up ¾ of the sides. Spoon 1-1⅓ teaspoons mascarpone into each mini-muffin cup; don't fill over the rim. Top each with about ½ teaspoon chopped pistachios and press lightly into mascarpone.

4 Bake for 9-11 minutes or until top rim of dough is golden brown. Let sit for 10 minutes to cool and gently remove using a knife inserted lightly along the outside edge of each cookie. Transfer to a cooling rack. Repeat until all dough and filling are used.

Yields about 3 dozen

INGREDIENTS

¾ cup unsalted butter, softened
1 cup sugar
1 large egg
1 teaspoon maple extract
2 cups all-purpose flour
½ teaspoon baking powder
½ teaspoon salt
1 cup mascarpone
⅓ cup pistachio meats,
    roughly chopped

Shopping List

INGREDIENTS

½ cup ricotta cheese
½ cup small-curd cottage cheese
1 tablespoon sour cream
1 tablespoon honey (or agave nectar)
2 tablespoons lemon juice
2 tablespoons lemon zest, divided
½ cup unsalted butter, softened
¼ cup sugar
1 cup all-purpose flour, divided
½ teaspoon ground ginger
½ teaspoon black pepper

FOR TOPPING

½ cup ricotta cheese
2 teaspoons honey (or agave nectar)
2 teaspoons lemon juice
12-15 fresh blackberries
12-15 fresh cherry halves

——— SMART COOKIE

To make this recipe with only one fruit (24-30 berries or cherries total), do not divide crust mixture and increase the black pepper (for blackberries) or ginger (for cherries) to 1 teaspoon. Another interesting combination: cinnamon and blueberries/mandarin orange.

NOUVEAU

Ricotta cheese, lemon, with blackberry and pepper, or cherry and ginger

A fresh twist on cheesecake, *Nouveau* is a mouthful of fruit and cheese that's both tangy and creamy. The spices in the light crust add a wonderful depth of flavor to each bite, while also sweetening gossip time with friends.

Pairing: Sparkling Wine

1 Preheat oven to 375° F. In a medium bowl, mix together ricotta cheese, cottage cheese, sour cream, honey, lemon juice and 1 tablespoon lemon zest. Set aside.

2 In a medium bowl, using an electric mixer, cream together butter, sugar and remaining 1 tablespoon lemon zest until light and fluffy, about 3 minutes. Divide mixture evenly into 2 bowls.

3 Stir together ½ cup flour and ½ teaspoon ginger, then add to butter mixture in one bowl. Beat until just incorporated. Next, stir together remaining ½ cup flour and ½ teaspoon black pepper, then add to butter mixture in remaining bowl. Beat until just incorporated.

Shopping List

4 Using each bowl of crust mixture, scoop or drop dough by 1 teaspoon portions and press into a nonstick or lightly buttered 24-cup mini-muffin pan. Press dough so it covers the bottom and half of the sides, with a recessed center. (Each bowl should fill 12 mini-muffin cups.) Spoon 1 rounded teaspoon of the cheese mixture into each mini-muffin cup. Keep in mind which mini-muffin cups have the ginger or black pepper crusts. Bake for 8-10 minutes or until top edges are just golden. Let sit for 15 minutes to cool and gently remove using a knife inserted lightly along the outside edge of each cookie. Transfer to a cooling rack.

5 In a small bowl, mix together ricotta cheese, honey and lemon juice until smooth. Spread ½ teaspoon cheese mixture onto each cookie and "frost." Then lightly press a blackberry on each black pepper-crusted cookie and a cherry half on each ginger-crusted cookie. Refrigerate any extra cookies.

Yields about 2 dozen

À L'ORANGE
Orange, cashew and mint

Fresh orange and mint might have been created just to lighten up the day. Paired with the crunch of a cashew, these flavors make up this summerlike cookie that registers negative in calories. Not because it has no calories, but because its taste will lead you to walk, dance, laugh and follow other invigorating activities . . . toward a lightness of being.

Pairing: Iced Tea

INGREDIENTS

¾ cup unsalted butter, softened
¾ cup sugar
1 large egg
1 teaspoon mint extract
1 tablespoon orange juice
1 tablespoon, plus ⅓ cup, orange zest, divided
2¼ cups all-purpose flour
1 teaspoon baking powder
½ teaspoon baking soda
¼ teaspoon salt
3 cups roasted cashews, finely chopped (salted or unsalted)
⅓ cup fresh mint leaves, finely chopped

1 In a large bowl, using an electric mixer, cream together butter and sugar until light and fluffy, about 3 minutes. Mix in egg, mint extract, orange juice and 1 tablespoon orange zest. Beat until well blended.

2 Whisk together flour, baking powder, baking soda and salt in a small bowl and add to butter mixture. Beat until just incorporated.

3 Form dough into 2 logs (1 inch in diameter) and wrap each in parchment paper. Freeze for 30 minutes or refrigerate for 2 hours.

4 Preheat oven to 350° F. In a small bowl, stir together cashews, chopped mint and remaining ⅓ cup orange zest. Slice logs into ¼-inch-thick rounds and lightly press each cookie, top and bottom, and roll sides into the nut mixture. Then place 1 inch apart on a parchment-lined or nonstick baking sheet. Bake for 10-12 minutes or until bottoms are golden brown. Let sit for a few minutes and transfer to a cooling rack.

Yields about 4 dozen

Shopping List

Cookie *ManCookie*

Pairing *Beer*

Page *49*

Cookie *Collaboration*

Pairing *Gewürztraminer*

Page *109*

Cookie *Dark Desire*

Pairing *Port*

Page *56*

Cookie *Crave*

Pairing *Coffee*

Page *119*

Cookie *Nosh*

Pairing *Amber Ale*

Page *130*

Cookie Interlude

Pairing Rosé

Page 51

Cookie Sweet Kebab

Pairing Sauvignon Blanc

Page 122

Cookie Three-Way

Pairing Pinot Grigio

Page 60

Cookie Refrescante

Pairing Margarita

Page 45

INDULGE
Mango and fresh ginger

A full bite of mango resting on a ginger cookie, *Indulge* offers an explosion of flavor followed by a tickling of heat. This cookie is much like a great conversation with your best friend — a little sweet and a little spicy. Indulge will awaken and delight the palate.

Pairing: Pinot Gris

INGREDIENTS

1 (5-inch) piece fresh ginger root, peeled (divided, see instructions)
¾ cup unsalted butter, softened
1 cup sugar
1 large egg
¼ cup molasses
2 cups all-purpose flour
½ teaspoon ground cinnamon
1 teaspoon baking soda
¼ teaspoon salt
1 mango, pitted and peeled (see instructions)

1 Using a microplane zester, finely grate enough ginger to yield 1½ teaspoons. Set aside grated ginger and remaining ginger root. In a large bowl, using an electric mixer, cream together butter and sugar until light and fluffy, about 3 minutes. Mix in egg, molasses and 1½ teaspoons grated ginger. Beat until well blended.

2 Whisk together flour, cinnamon, baking soda and salt in a small bowl and add to butter mixture. Beat until just incorporated.

3 Form dough into 2 logs (1¼ inches in diameter) and wrap each in parchment paper. Roll logs on counter to form a consistent round shape. Freeze for 30 minutes or refrigerate for 2 hours.

4 Slice peeled mango into 48 bite-sized pieces (each approximately 1 inch square by ⅛ inch-thick). Refrigerate any leftover mango. Set aside pieces. Using remaining ginger root, cut ginger into 48 slivers (each approximately ½ inch long by ¼ inch-thick).

Shopping List

5 Preheat oven to 350° F. Slice logs into ¼-inch-thick rounds (⅛-inch-thick for a crunchier cookie) and place 1½ inches apart on a parchment-lined or nonstick baking sheet. On each cookie, place a mango slice and pierce center of the mango slice and cookie with a knife point. Then place a sliver of ginger into the piercing, lengthwise, so it goes through the mango and cookie, and a small amount sticks out above the mango (see photo for reference). Bake for 10-12 minutes or until bottoms are just golden. Let sit for a few minutes and transfer to a cooling rack.

Yields about 4 dozen

TRADITION

Dried plum, allspice, cinnamon, black pepper and walnut

These are flavors I grew up with in California's Santa Clara Valley. That was before it became known as Silicon Valley. *Tradition* reminds me of fruit and nut flavors of my past. When paired with the golden warmth of brandy, these cookies are perfect to share while reminiscing with old friends about good times growing up.

Pairing: Brandy

INGREDIENTS

¾ cup unsalted butter, softened
1½ cups light brown sugar, packed
3 large eggs
1 tablespoon vanilla extract
2 cups dried plums, roughly chopped
2¾ cups all-purpose flour
½ teaspoon allspice
1½ teaspoons ground cinnamon
½ teaspoon black pepper
½ teaspoon baking soda
¼ teaspoon salt
1 cup walnuts, chopped (optional,
    not in photo)

1 Preheat oven to 350° F. In a large bowl, using an electric mixer, cream together butter and brown sugar until light and fluffy, about 3 minutes. Mix in eggs, 1 at a time, until thoroughly blended. Add vanilla and dried plums. Beat until well blended.

2 Whisk together flour, allspice, cinnamon, black pepper, baking soda and salt in a small bowl and add to butter mixture. Beat until just incorporated. Fold in walnuts, if using.

3 Scoop or drop dough by 1 teaspoon portions and place 1½ inches apart on a parchment-lined or nonstick baking sheet. Bake for 7-9 minutes or until bottoms are light brown. Let sit for a few minutes and transfer to a cooling rack.

Yields about 5 dozen

Shopping List

AFTERNOON
Prune, Earl Grey tea and lemon

A quiet blend of fragrant tea and lemon, *Afternoon* offers a ray of sunshine and contrast in texture. Prunes satisfy the palate, please the body and deserve our recognition as delightful components of cookies for grown-ups.

Pairing: Hot Tea or Merlot

1 Place prunes, lemon sections and tea bags in a saucepan. Cover with water. On medium-low heat, bring mixture to a simmer (do not boil) for 5 minutes. Set aside. Spoon out lemons and prunes, place on a paper towel to dry. Leave tea bags in the water and set aside.

2 Preheat oven to 375° F. In a large bowl, using an electric mixer, cream together butter and sugar until light and fluffy, about 3 minutes. Mix in eggs, 1 at a time, until thoroughly blended. Add lemon juice and cream cheese. Beat until well blended.

3 Whisk together flour, baking soda and salt in a small bowl and add to butter mixture. Beat until just incorporated.

4 Scoop or drop dough by 1 rounded teaspoon portions, form into balls, flatten to ¼ inch-thick and place 1½ inches apart on a parchment-lined or nonstick baking sheet. Place half a prune onto each cookie, along with a lemon section. Bake for 8-10 minutes or until bottoms are a light golden brown. Let sit for a few minutes and transfer to a cooling rack.

5 To make glaze: In a separate bowl, mix confectioners' sugar, honey, lemon juice, and 3 tablespoons tea/water mixture until a glaze consistency is formed. Add a little more tea/water mixture to the glaze, if needed for consistency. Brush or drizzle glaze over each cookie.

Yields about 5 dozen

INGREDIENTS

36 prunes, halved
2 lemons, peeled and sectioned
2 bags Earl Grey tea
½ cup unsalted butter, softened
1 cup sugar
2 large eggs
1½ teaspoons lemon juice
3 ounces cream cheese, softened
2¾ cups all-purpose flour
½ teaspoon baking soda
¼ teaspoon salt

FOR GLAZE
1½ cups confectioners' sugar, sifted
2 tablespoons honey
2 tablespoons lemon juice
3 tablespoons Earl Grey tea water

Shopping List

INGREDIENTS

1 cup unsalted butter, softened
⅔ cup sugar
½ cup confectioners' sugar, sifted
2 egg yolks
2 tablespoons lemon juice
2 tablespoons lemon zest
1 tablespoon orange liqueur
4 tablespoons vodka
6 tablespoons raw sugar, divided
2⅔ cups all-purpose flour
½ teaspoon baking powder
¼ teaspoon salt

FOR FROSTING

3 tablespoons unsalted butter, softened
2 cups confectioners' sugar, sifted
2 tablespoons vodka
3 tablespoons lemon juice
1 tablespoon orange liqueur
Mint leaves, for decoration (optional)

'TINI

Lemon, vodka, orange liqueur and sugar

Inspired by a lemon drop martini, 'Tini is just as light and addicting as its alter ego. 'Tini is served best with friends, laughs and stories of wild times. Soft and crunchy. Sour and sweet. Much like life.

Pairing: Lemon Vodka with Club Soda

1 In a large bowl, using an electric mixer, cream together butter and sugars until light and fluffy, about 3 minutes. Mix in egg yolks, lemon juice and zest, orange liqueur, vodka and 3 tablespoons raw sugar. Beat until well blended.

2 Whisk together flour, baking powder and salt in a small bowl and add to butter mixture. Beat until just incorporated.

3 Form dough into 2 logs (1 inch in diameter) and wrap each in parchment paper. Flatten sides of logs to form the triangular shape of a martini glass. Freeze for 1 hour or refrigerate for 3 hours.

4 Preheat oven to 350° F. Cut logs into ¼-inch-thick slices (exaggerate martini shape by trimming with a knife). Place the remaining 3 tablespoons raw sugar on a plate and press the edges of each cookie into sugar to coat. Place each 1 inch apart on a parchment-lined or nonstick baking sheet. Bake for 11-13 minutes or until bottoms are just golden. Let sit for a few minutes and transfer to a cooling rack.

5 To make frosting, mix together butter, confectioners' sugar, vodka, lemon juice and orange liqueur until a consistency between a frosting and a glaze forms. Frost cookies, leaving ¼ inch border around the edges. It should not cover the raw sugar edges of the cookie. If using, decorate each with a small portion of a mint leaf.

Yields about 5 dozen

Shopping List

HEARTBEET

Beet, feta cheese and lemon thyme

I'm a bit obsessed with cooking with root vegetables. Inspiration for this cookie came from the bistro beet salads friends and I ordered at lunch escapes from work. *Heartbeet* balances the earthiness of baked beets and fresh lemon thyme with feta cheese, and a little more lemon thyme.

Pairing: Chardonnay

1 Preheat oven to 400° F. Trim roots and greens from beets. Wrap whole beets in aluminum foil with a drizzle of olive oil and lemon thyme sprigs. Bake for 1 hour. Cool; discard baked thyme and peel beets. Set aside.

2 Lower oven temperature to 350° F. In a large bowl, using an electric mixer, cream together butter and sugars until light and fluffy, about 3 minutes. Mix in egg, lemon zest and lemon thyme. Beat until well blended.

3 Whisk together flour, baking soda and salt in a small bowl and add to butter mixture. Beat until just incorporated.

4 Coarsely grate the baked beets. Fold 1 cup grated beets and feta into dough.

5 Scoop or drop dough by 1 teaspoon portions and place 1½ inches apart on a parchment-lined or nonstick baking sheet. Bake for 10-12 minutes or until bottoms are light brown. Let sit for a few minutes and transfer to a cooling rack.

Yields about 5 dozen

INGREDIENTS

2 large (or 3 medium) fresh beets
1 tablespoon olive oil
1-2 sprigs fresh lemon thyme*
½ cup unsalted butter, softened
½ cup light brown sugar, packed
½ cup sugar
1 large egg
2 tablespoons lemon zest
2 tablespoons fresh lemon thyme, finely chopped (can substitute fresh thyme)
2 cups all-purpose flour
1 teaspoon baking soda
½ teaspoon coarse salt
½ cup feta cheese, crumbled

SMART COOKIE

Lemon thyme is a flavorful herb that should be available at your local spice shop or specialty store. If you cannot find it, when you bake the beets substitute fresh thyme and a few lemon slices.

Shopping List

INGREDIENTS

½ cup unsalted butter, softened

1 cup sugar

1 large egg

1 tablespoon lime zest

2 tablespoons lime juice

1 teaspoon vanilla extract

1 tablespoon fresh ginger root,
   finely grated*

1 tablespoon fresh jalapeno,
   finely grated*

1¾ cups all-purpose flour

½ teaspoon baking powder

½ teaspoon salt

SMART COOKIE

*To really make the ginger and
jalapeno flavors pop, grate them
using a microplane zester.*

CROOKIE
Fresh ginger, jalapeno and lime

Fresh, hot soup. Served with bread or crackers again? Try the *Crookie* instead, a fragrant, savory treat that's crisp outside, yet soft in the center. The dough freezes well, and can be sliced and baked as your soup heats. Today's soups have transformed into alluring combinations of vegetables and spices. Isn't it time to transform the accompaniment, as well?

Pairing: Hot Ginger Tea or Pinot Noir

1 In a large bowl, using an electric mixer, cream together butter and sugar until light and fluffy, about 3 minutes. Mix in egg, lime zest and juice, vanilla, ginger and jalapeno. Beat until well blended.

2 Whisk together flour, baking powder and salt in a small bowl and add to butter mixture. Beat until just incorporated.

3 Form dough into a log (1½ inches in diameter) and wrap in parchment paper. Press log on counter to form a square shape. Freeze for 30 minutes or refrigerate for 2 hours.

4 Preheat oven to 350° F. Slice log into ⅛-inch-thick squares, cut each in half crosswise to form a triangle, and place 1 inch apart on a parchment-lined or nonstick baking sheet. Bake for 7-9 minutes or until bottoms are golden brown. Let sit for a few minutes and transfer to a cooling rack.

Yields about 4 dozen

Shopping List

MEDITERRANEAN
Feta cheese, dill, sun-dried tomato and lemon

Delicious with iced drinks on a warm afternoon or as a satisfying, savory cookie before — or after — a meal, *Mediterranean* captures distinct flavors in a light, crumbly cookie that delights in appearance, taste and texture. Consider it inspiration to plan a Mediterranean vacation with friends.

Pairing: Lemonade

INGREDIENTS

¾ cup unsalted butter, softened
¾ cup sugar
1 large egg
1 teaspoon vanilla extract
1 tablespoon lemon zest
   (Meyer lemon preferred)
1 tablespoon lemon juice
   (Meyer lemon preferred)
3 tablespoons fresh dill,
   chopped medium
2 cups all-purpose flour
½ teaspoon baking soda
¼ teaspoon salt
⅓ cup feta cheese, crumbled
½ cup sun-dried tomatoes,
   roughly chopped

1 In a large bowl, using an electric mixer, cream together butter and sugar until light and fluffy, about 3 minutes. Mix in egg, vanilla, lemon zest and juice, and dill. Beat until well blended.

2 Whisk together flour, baking soda and salt in a small bowl and add to butter mixture. Beat until just incorporated. Stir in feta cheese and sun-dried tomatoes.

3 Form dough into a log (1½ inches in diameter) and wrap in parchment paper. Roll log on counter to form a consistent round shape. Freeze for 30 minutes or refrigerate for 2 hours.

4 Preheat oven to 350° F. Slice log into ¼-inch-thick rounds and place 1½ inches apart on a parchment-lined or nonstick baking sheet. Bake for 10-12 minutes or until bottoms are just golden. Let sit for a few minutes and transfer to a cooling rack.

Yields about 4 dozen

Shopping List

COOKIE MARY

Tomato, vodka, lemon, lime, curry, Tabasco® and Worcestershire

Created with a Bloody Mary cocktail in mind, this mouthful of flavor wakes up the taste buds. Serve this chewy treat with great conversation at a brunch or lunch with your girlfriends; no need for the real thing when you can devour this cookie version.

Pairing: Coffee

1 Preheat oven to 350° F. In a large bowl, using an electric mixer, cream together butter and sugars until light and fluffy, about 3 minutes. Mix in egg, tomato juice, Worcestershire sauce, horseradish, curry powder, Tabasco® and vodka. Beat until well blended.

2 Whisk together flour, baking soda and salt in a small bowl and add to butter mixture. Beat until just incorporated.

3 Scoop or drop dough by 1 rounded teaspoon portions and place 1 inch apart on a parchment-lined or nonstick baking sheet. Bake for 20-23 minutes or until bottoms begin to brown. Let sit for a few minutes and transfer to a cooling rack.

4 For frosting: In a medium bowl, mix together butter, zests and tomato juice. Add in confectioners' sugar and mix to a creamy frosting consistency. Frost cookies. Sprinkle ground pepper over each cookie.

Yields about 3 dozen

Shopping List

INGREDIENTS

½ cup unsalted butter, softened
½ cup sugar
½ cup light brown sugar, packed
1 large egg
3 tablespoons tomato juice
½ teaspoon Worcestershire sauce
½ teaspoon horseradish
½ teaspoon curry powder
2-3 dashes Tabasco®
3 tablespoons vodka
2 cups all-purpose flour
½ teaspoon baking soda
½ teaspoon salt

FOR FROSTING
2 tablespoons unsalted butter, softened
1 teaspoon lime zest
1 teaspoon lemon zest
¼ cup tomato juice
2 cups confectioners' sugar, sifted
1 tablespoon tri-colored peppercorns
   (or black), coarsely ground

Chapter 6

Guys' Night In

Telling stories about past adventures or planning new ones or even just catching up can make a guy's night at home (or at his buddy's place) even better! These cookies will satisfy a man-sized appetite.

NOSTALGIA

Pecan, brown sugar, molasses, rosemary, thyme, cayenne and maple

As a child, I remember seeing and smelling sticky buns at county fairs on the way to our exhibits or livestock. Those days of 4-H and Future Farmers of America made for great memories; this cookie revives tradition as it updates taste. Flavorful and moist, *Nostalgia* is reminiscent of those wonderful sticky buns, yet renewed with an herb-and-maple base.

Pairing: Iced Tea

1 Preheat oven to 375° F. In a large bowl, using an electric mixer, cream together butter and sugar until light and fluffy, about 3 minutes. Mix in egg, maple extract and molasses. Beat until well blended.

2 Whisk together flour, rosemary, thyme, cayenne, baking soda and salt in a small bowl and add to butter mixture. Beat until just incorporated.

3 To make topping: In a separate bowl, mix together butter, brown sugar and honey. Stir in pecans. Set aside.

4 Scoop or drop dough by 1 rounded teaspoon portions, roll into balls, and place 1 inch apart on a parchment-lined or nonstick baking sheet. Press each to ¼ inch-thickness. Using the topping mixture, form balls (½ inch in diameter) and lightly press one onto the center of each cookie. Bake for 9-10 minutes or until bottoms are golden brown. (Bake an additional minute for a crisper cookie.) Let sit for a few minutes and transfer to a cooling rack.

Yields about 5 dozen

Shopping List

INGREDIENTS

⅔ cup unsalted butter, softened
¾ cup light brown sugar, packed
1 large egg
1 teaspoon maple extract
½ cup molasses
2¾ cups all-purpose flour
1 teaspoon fresh rosemary, chopped medium
1 teaspoon fresh thyme, chopped medium
⅛ teaspoon cayenne pepper
1 teaspoon baking soda
¼ teaspoon salt

FOR TOPPING
¼ cup unsalted butter, softened
¾ cup light brown sugar, packed
1 tablespoon honey
¾ cup pecans, roughly chopped

CHEWY

Ricotta cheese, tangerine, cardamom, cranberry and Marcona almond

It's great fun to experiment with different sensory combinations and consider the experiences they evoke. *Chewy* was inspired by an article I read about the quest for a chewy food that lingers in the mouth a moment longer than a soft or crisp morsel. The texture of a chewy cookie with the addition of nuts and dried fruit creates this satisfying result.

Pairing: Tangerine Tea

INGREDIENTS

½ cup unsalted butter, softened
1 cup sugar
1 large egg
1 cup part-skim ricotta cheese
2 tablespoons tangerine juice
½ teaspoon tangerine zest
1¼ cups all-purpose flour
½ teaspoon ground cardamom
½ teaspoon baking powder
½ teaspoon salt
1¼ cups dried cranberries
½ cup Marcona almonds,
    chopped medium

1 Preheat oven to 350° F. In a large bowl, using an electric mixer, cream together butter and sugar until light and fluffy, about 3 minutes. Mix in egg, ricotta cheese and tangerine juice and zest. Beat until well blended.

2 Whisk together flour, cardamom, baking powder and salt in a small bowl and add to butter mixture. Beat until just incorporated. Stir in cranberries and almonds.

3 Scoop or drop dough by 1 teaspoon portions and place 1 inch apart on a parchment-lined or nonstick baking sheet. Bake for 10-12 minutes or until bottoms are just golden. Let sit for a few minutes and transfer to a cooling rack.

Yields about 3 dozen

Shopping List

AT THE DINER

Yukon Gold potato, onion, sausage and chive

Inspired by a traditional diner breakfast of eggs, sausage, potatoes and a biscuit, *At The Diner* brings to mind the hearty meals served when big appetites wake up on a weekend morning. These savory cookies bake up with a soft interior from the sausage and potatoes and a nice exterior crust. Leftover sausage, potatoes or bacon will also work well in this recipe.

Pairing: Coffee

1 In a sauté pan over medium heat, fry sausage until it is cooked. Remove from pan and set aside. Drain oil from pan, leaving 2 tablespoons (or heat 2 tablespoons olive oil in a fresh pan) and sauté potatoes and onion until cooked but not quite soft. Set aside to cool.

2 Preheat oven to 425° F. Whisk together flour, sugar, baking powder, baking soda and salt in a large bowl. Gently stir in melted butter. Use fingers to create consistent dough with as little handling as possible (it will be fluffier when not overworked). Gently fold milk into the dough, using fingers to mix. Once the milk is incorporated, fold in sausage, potatoes and onion.

3 Scoop or drop dough by 1 teaspoon portions and place 1 inch apart on a parchment-lined or nonstick baking sheet. Lightly brush tops of cookies with egg and sprinkle with a few chives. Bake for 15 minutes or until bottoms and edges are golden. Let sit for a few minutes and transfer to a cooling rack.

Yields about 5 dozen

Shopping List

INGREDIENTS

- 1 cup breakfast sausage, crumbled patties or links, roughly chopped
- 2 tablespoons olive oil
- 1 cup Yukon Gold potatoes, chopped into small cubes, unpeeled or peeled
- ¼ cup onion, finely chopped
- 1¾ cups all-purpose flour
- 2 tablespoons sugar
- 1 teaspoon baking powder
- ½ teaspoon baking soda
- ½ teaspoon salt
- ½ cup unsalted or salted butter, melted
- 1 cup milk or buttermilk
- 2 large eggs, slightly beaten
- 2 tablespoons chives, chopped medium

ON A SPICY DATE
Jalapeno jack cheese, cornmeal, fresh date and cream cheese

Inspired by the shape of an empanada, *On a Spicy Date's* cheesy corn taste goes well with a cold beer. The fresh date inside adds a sweetness to counter the cookie's spiciness.

Pairing: Mexican Lager

INGREDIENTS

½ cup unsalted butter, softened
8 ounces jalapeno jack cheese, grated
⅔ cup all-purpose flour
⅓ cup cornmeal
½ teaspoon cayenne pepper
½ teaspoon coarse salt
12-15 fresh dates, pitted and
    quartered (can substitute dried)
3 ounces cream cheese, softened

1 Preheat oven to 300° F. In a large bowl, stir together butter and grated cheese.

2 Whisk together flour, cornmeal, cayenne and salt in a small bowl and add to butter mixture. Mix until just incorporated.

3 Thinly roll out dough and cut rounds using a 2-inch circular cookie cutter or a glass (or using 1 teaspoon dough for each, create thin, 2-inch rounds with your fingers). The thinner the dough, the more pronounced the date flavor will be.

4 Place 2 quarters of a date lengthwise, across the diameter of the cookie. Add ½ teaspoon cream cheese to each cookie, ¼ teaspoon tucked into each of the two date pieces if possible. Fold the dough over the date to form a semi-circle with the two date pieces inside. Press the outside edges of the cookie together and use the tines of a fork to create an empanada-style edge.

5 Place each 1 inch apart on a parchment-lined or nonstick baking sheet. Bake for 30 minutes or until edges are just golden. Let sit for a few minutes and transfer to a cooling rack.

Yields about 2 dozen

Shopping List

COOL
Cucum[...]

Cool As A [...]
One dou[...]
and lemo[...]
cucumbe[...]

1 In a [...]
  until [...]

2 Whi[...]
  butte[...]
bowls.

3 In or[...]
  low s[...]
molasses [...]
Form eac[...]
in parchm[...]

4 Preh[...]
  1½ i[...]
¼ teaspoc[...]
minutes [...]
transfer t[...]

5 To m[...]
  cucu[...]
red peppe[...]

Yields ab[...]

HIT-THE-SPOT
Pretzel, Cheddar cheese and mustard

Sometimes it takes a pretzel to satisfy a salt craving. And, what's a pretzel without mustard? Then again, cheese and pretzels taste great together, too. Can a pretzel be in a cookie? *Hit-the-Spot* has the answers. It envelops all these ingredients into a delicious cookie that reassures us pretzels do have a place in the cookie realm.

Pairing: Stout

1 Preheat oven to 375° F. In a large bowl, using an electric mixer, cream together butter and sugar until light and fluffy, about 3 minutes. Mix in egg and vanilla. Beat until well blended.

2 Whisk together flour, baking powder and salt in a small bowl and add to butter mixture. Beat until just incorporated. Fold in pretzels.

3 Scoop or drop dough by 1 rounded tablespoon portions and place 1½ inches apart on a parchment-lined or nonstick baking sheet. Press the top of each to create a flat surface. Then on each cookie, place ½ teaspoon mustard, a slice of cheese and a mini pretzel. Bake for 8-10 minutes or until bottoms are golden brown. Let sit for a few minutes and transfer to a cooling rack.

Yields about 4 dozen

Shopping List

INGREDIENTS

¾ cup unsalted butter, softened
1 cup sugar
1 large egg
1 teaspoon vanilla
2 cups all-purpose flour
½ teaspoon baking powder
¼ teaspoon salt
1 cup pretzels, roughly chopped

FOR TOPPING

½ cup prepared mustard, spicy brown (or your favorite)
48 (¾-inch-square) slices Cheddar cheese
48 mini pretzels

FETTUCCINE

Egg noodle, cream, Parmesan, pecan and nutmeg

One path to creating recipes for *Cookies for Grown-ups* was to ask friends about their favorite foods. After the second vote for fettuccine, I thought it would be fun to bite into an egg noodle with a creamy center and dash of nutmeg. The pecan crust adds a depth of flavor and a little crunch.

Pairing: Chardonnay

INGREDIENTS

½ cup unsalted butter, softened
¼ cup light brown sugar, packed
1 large egg yolk
½ teaspoon vanilla
½ cup all-purpose flour
¼ teaspoon nutmeg
¼ teaspoon baking powder
¼ teaspoon salt
½ cup pecans, chopped medium

FOR FILLING

4 cups water
¾ cup medium egg noodles
¼ teaspoon salt
1 teaspoon unsalted butter, softened
2 tablespoons shallots, finely chopped
8 ounces cream cheese, softened
⅓ cup heavy cream
1 cup grated Parmesan cheese
½ teaspoon salt
½ teaspoon pepper
1 teaspoon nutmeg

1 Preheat oven to 350° F. In a large bowl, using an electric mixer, cream together butter and sugar until light and fluffy, about 3 minutes. Mix in egg yolk and vanilla.

2 Whisk together flour, nutmeg, baking powder, salt and pecans in a small bowl and add to butter mixture. Beat until just incorporated. Refrigerate dough for 30 minutes.

3 Scoop or drop dough by ¾ teaspoon portions and press into 2 nonstick or lightly buttered 24-cup mini-muffin pans. Press dough so it covers the bottom and creates a small rim up the sides, with a recessed center. Do not fill the muffin tins or bring the dough up the full height of the side. Bake for 5 minutes. Set aside.

4 In a saucepan, bring 4 cups water to a boil. Add noodles and salt. Boil for 8 minutes or until soft. Rinse with cold water, drain, and set aside.

5 In a skillet, melt butter over medium-low heat and sauté shallots for 3 minutes. Reduce heat to low and stir in cream cheese, heavy cream, Parmesan, salt and pepper; cook for 3 minutes. Drop 1-1½ teaspoons of the cheese mixture into each muffin cup (they will be not quite full). Lay 2 noodles onto each so they curl and stay on the cheese mixture surface. Sprinkle each with a pinch of nutmeg. Bake for 15-18 minutes or until edges are golden. Let sit for 20 minutes to cool, then gently remove with the help of a knife inserted lightly along the outside edge of each cookie. Transfer to a cooling rack.

Yields about 3 dozen

KICKIN'

Green apple, horseradish and fresh ginger

Zing! Pow! Wow. *Kickin'* wakes up the taste buds with a combination of tang and heat. Complementary sweet and savory flavors surprise, but don't overwhelm in this fun morsel. Use fresh or prepared horseradish, either work.

Pairing: Ginger Tea

INGREDIENTS

½ cup unsalted butter, softened
¾ cup light brown sugar, packed
1 large egg
1 teaspoon vanilla extract
2 cups Golden Delicious apples, unpeeled and cored, finely chopped
½ cup sour cream
2 tablespoons horseradish
2 teaspoons fresh ginger root, finely grated
1¾ cups all-purpose flour
⅓ cup cornmeal
½ teaspoon baking powder
½ teaspoon salt

1 Preheat oven to 375° F. In a large bowl, using an electric mixer, cream together butter and sugar until light and fluffy, about 3 minutes. Mix in egg until thoroughly blended. Add in vanilla extract, apples, sour cream, horseradish and ginger. Beat until well blended.

2 Whisk together flour, cornmeal, baking powder and salt in a small bowl and add to butter mixture. Beat until just incorporated.

3 Scoop or drop dough by 1 rounded teaspoon portions and place 1½ inches apart on a parchment-lined or nonstick baking sheet. Bake for 7-9 minutes or until bottoms are golden. Let sit for a few minutes and transfer to a cooling rack.

Yields about 5 dozen

Shopping List

COOKIE SHOT
Lime, tequila, and a little more tequila

Are you a fan of tequila with lime? Have a shot at any time of day — a *Cookie Shot*. A reminder of the unique flavors that can be experienced beyond a bar with a beer chaser. Inspired by sharing the taste of tequila with friends, *Cookie Shot* brings a smile to the idea of celebration. Use a tequila you enjoy, the cookie will carry the nuance of that taste.

Pairing: Mexican Pale Lager

1. In a large bowl, using an electric mixer, cream together butter and sugar until light and fluffy, about 3 minutes. Mix in tequila, lime zest and juice.

2. Whisk together flour and cornstarch in a small bowl and add to butter mixture. Beat until just incorporated.

3. Form dough into 2 logs (1½ inches in diameter) and wrap each in parchment paper. Freeze for 30 minutes or refrigerate for 2 hours.

4. Preheat oven to 350° F. Slice logs into ¼-inch-thick rounds and place 1 inch apart on a parchment-lined or nonstick baking sheet. Bake for 15 minutes or until bottoms are golden brown. Let sit for a few minutes and transfer to a cooling rack.

5. To make glaze: In a small bowl, whisk confectioners' sugar, lime zest and tequila to a glaze consistency. Brush cookies with glaze and top each with a thin lime slice.

Yields about 4 dozen

Shopping List

INGREDIENTS

¾ cup unsalted butter
⅓ cup confectioners' sugar, sifted
¼ cup tequila
1 tablespoon lime zest
1 tablespoon lime juice
2 cups all-purpose flour
2 tablespoons cornstarch

FOR GLAZE AND TOPPING

1 cup confectioners' sugar, sifted
1 teaspoon lime zest
3 tablespoons tequila
2 limes, peeled and cut into thin slices and quartered

Chapter 7

I Want to Say . . .

Thank you. Happy Birthday. Congratulations. Feel better. *Cookies for Grown-ups* respects the efforts of others in our work and personal lives. This chapter salutes special occasions of colleagues and friends or says, "I want to say I am thinking of you."

RETREAT
Pineapple, banana, coconut, fresh ginger and walnut

An afternoon visit to a tropical island may be out of the question but a retreat into your imagination with a few bites of sun and fun is wholly possible. *Retreat* reflects both a fruity umbrella drink and a sweet, yet tangy, dessert — perfect when eaten on a porch on a warm, balmy day. Let these cookies be your sunny wish for a friend stuck in a cold place.

Pairing: Pineapple Juice on Ice

1. Preheat oven to 350° F. Lightly butter the bottom and sides of a 9-by-13-inch baking dish. Set aside. In a large bowl, using an electric mixer, cream together butter and sugar until light and fluffy, about 3 minutes. Mix in coconut extract.

2. Whisk together flour and salt in a small bowl and add to butter mixture. Beat until just incorporated. Stir in pecans.

3. Press dough into prepared pan. Bake for 20 minutes. Leave oven on and set pan aside to cool a bit while preparing topping.

4. In a bowl, stir together melted butter, pineapple, banana, coconut, walnuts, lemon juice and ginger. Sprinkle flour over top and stir in. Spread the mixture over cookie base. Bake for 25 minutes. Test with a knife in the center of top dough. It should be moist, not doughy; the edges will be bubbled, not dry. Let cool for 15 minutes. Cut into 1½-inch squares and serve. Refrigerate any extra portions.

Yields about 4 dozen

Shopping List

INGREDIENTS

¾ cup unsalted butter, softened
⅓ cup sugar
1 teaspoon coconut extract
2¼ cups all-purpose flour
¼ teaspoon salt
½ cup pecans, chopped medium

FOR TOPPING

1 tablespoon unsalted butter, melted
1 cup pineapple, roughly chopped
¾ cup mashed banana
¾ cup shredded coconut, toasted
¾ cup walnuts, chopped medium
1 tablespoon lemon juice
1 tablespoon fresh ginger root, minced
1 tablespoon all-purpose flour

PINK-A-DOT
Pink grapefruit and poppy seed

I love pink grapefruit and had fun finding its perfect role in a cookie. *Pink-a-Dot* is both crisp and soft. The poppy seeds add spots of personality, and the light glaze doesn't have the sugary blast of a frosting. These cookies are wonderful with an afternoon tea or as part of a birthday celebration.

Pairing: Club Soda & Splash of Pomegranate Juice

INGREDIENTS

¾ cup unsalted butter, softened
1 cup sugar
3 tablespoons grapefruit zest
¼ cup fresh grapefruit juice
1 teaspoon vanilla extract
2 cups all-purpose flour
½ teaspoon baking powder
¼ teaspoon salt
2 teaspoons poppy seeds

FOR GLAZE

1 cup confectioners' sugar, sifted
1 teaspoon grapefruit zest
3 tablespoons fresh grapefruit juice

1 In a large bowl, using an electric mixer, cream together butter and sugar until light and fluffy, about 3 minutes. Mix in grapefruit zest and juice, and vanilla. Beat until well blended.

2 Whisk together flour, baking powder and salt in a small bowl and add to butter mixture. Beat until just incorporated. Fold in poppy seeds.

3 Form dough into logs (2 inches in diameter) and wrap each in parchment paper. Freeze for 30 minutes or refrigerate for 2 hours.

4 Preheat oven to 325° F. Slice logs into ⅛-inch-thick rounds and place 1½ inches apart on a parchment-lined or nonstick baking sheet. Bake for 13-15 minutes or until bottoms are light golden-brown. Let sit for a few minutes and transfer to a cooling rack.

5 To make glaze: In a small bowl, mix together confectioners' sugar, grapefruit zest and juice until you reach a glaze consistency. Paint a thin coating of glaze on top of each cookie.

Yields about 3 dozen

Shopping List

ENTICING

Blackberry, lemon, agave nectar, ricotta cheese and chocolate

This sweet treat mimics the texture of lasagna. Zesty fruit and smooth ricotta are layered within a soft chocolate cookie. *Enticing's* variety of textures invites and inspires you to explore flavors and, perhaps, eat a few more cookies than you intended.

| Pairing: Merlot

1 In a large bowl, using an electric mixer, cream together butter and sugar until light and fluffy, about 3 minutes. Mix in egg and vanilla. Beat until well blended.

2 Whisk together flour, cocoa powder, baking soda and salt in a small bowl and add to butter mixture. Beat until just incorporated.

3 Form dough into 2 logs (1½ inches in diameter) and wrap each in parchment paper. Freeze for 1 hour or refrigerate for 2 hours.

4 In a separate bowl, mix together blackberries, ricotta, cream cheese, lemon juice and zest and agave nectar. Set aside.

5 Preheat oven to 325° F. Slice logs into ⅛-inch-thick rounds. Using 2 nonstick or lightly buttered 24-cup mini-muffin pans, line the bottom and halfway up the sides of each cup with a dough slice. Top each with ½ teaspoon berry filling, then a half of a dough slice, followed by another ½ teaspoon berry filling, ending with a small triangle of dough. (Layers and shape of dough don't need to be exact. Don't overfill muffin cups.)

6 Bake for 15-16 minutes or until knife inserted comes out clean. Let sit for 15 minutes then gently remove with the help of a knife inserted lightly along the outside edge of each cookie. Transfer to a cooling rack.

Yields about 4 dozen

INGREDIENTS

1 cup unsalted butter, softened
1⅓ cups light brown sugar, packed
1 large egg
1 teaspoon vanilla extract
2½ cups all-purpose flour
⅓ cup unsweetened cocoa powder
¼ teaspoon baking soda
¼ teaspoon salt
1 cup blackberries, roughly chopped
1 cup ricotta cheese
4 ounces cream cheese, softened
3 tablespoons lemon juice
3 tablespoons lemon zest
3 tablespoons agave nectar

Shopping List

COFFEE BREAK
Dried fruit, nut and coffee

This afternoon pick-me-up is a tasty alternative to a vending-machine snack or candy bar. Take a batch to work for your well deserving coworkers. I make *Coffee Break* with dried figs and walnut, but the recipe works well with any of your favorite dried fruits and nuts.

Pairing: Coffee

INGREDIENTS

1 cup unsalted butter, softened
¾ cup sugar
½ cup light brown sugar, packed
1 large egg
1 teaspoon vanilla extract
2½ cups all-purpose flour
½ teaspoon baking powder
½ teaspoon baking soda
½ teaspoon salt
1½ cups dried figs, roughly chopped
¾ cup walnut halves

1 Preheat oven to 350° F. In a large bowl, using an electric mixer, cream together butter and sugars until light and fluffy, about 3 minutes. Mix in egg and vanilla. Beat until well blended.

2 Whisk together flour, baking powder, baking soda and salt in a small bowl and add to butter mixture. Beat until just incorporated. Fold in chopped figs.

3 Scoop or drop dough by 1 teaspoon portions and place 1½ inches apart on a parchment-lined or nonstick baking sheet. Place 1 walnut half on each cookie. Bake for 10-12 minutes or until bottoms begin to brown. Let sit for a few minutes and transfer to a cooling rack.

Yields about 5 dozen

Shopping List

TROPICAL COMFORT

Oat, mango, walnut and coconut

The homey taste of oatmeal combines with fresh mango and coconut in *Tropical Comfort*. A perfect hostess gift at a beach luau or a backyard picnic.

Pairing: Fruity Iced Tea

1 Preheat oven to 325° F. In a large bowl, using an electric mixer, cream together butter and sugars until light and fluffy, about 3 minutes. Beat in eggs, 1 at a time, until blended. Mix in mango and vanilla. Beat until well blended.

2 Whisk together flour, cinnamon, baking powder and salt in a small bowl and add to butter mixture. Beat until just incorporated. Fold in toasted coconut, oats, raisins and walnuts.

3 Scoop or drop dough by 1 teaspoon portions and place 1½ inches apart on a parchment-lined or nonstick baking sheet. Bake for 15 minutes or until bottoms are light golden brown. Let sit for a few minutes and transfer to a cooling rack.

Yields about 5 dozen

Shopping List

INGREDIENTS

1 cup unsalted butter, softened
¾ cup sugar
1 cup light brown sugar, packed
2 large eggs
1 medium mango, peeled and pitted, mashed (to yield 1 cup)
2 teaspoons vanilla extract
2 cups all-purpose flour
1 teaspoon ground cinnamon
1 teaspoon baking powder
1 teaspoon coarse salt
⅔ cup shredded coconut, toasted*
2 cups old-fashioned oats (not instant or quick-cooking)
⅔ cup golden raisins
⅔ cup chopped walnuts

SMART COOKIE

*If using shredded coconut, toast it in oven or on stovetop. To toast in oven, spread coconut in a thin layer on baking sheet. Bake at 300° F for about 20 minutes, stirring every 5 minutes to ensure coconut browns evenly. To toast on stovetop, spread coconut in a large skillet and cook over medium heat, stirring frequently until golden brown. Coconut burns easily so watch closely.

SUMMER DAYS
Dried apricot, caramel, hazelnut and orange zest

Inspired by my childhood summers in San José, California, *Summer Days* brings back memories of a valley of orchards full of apricots, oranges and nuts — and a bowl of soft caramel candies. It reminds me of days of baking, sewing and preparing animals for the county fair; these cookies also call to mind good friends and my first pick-up truck.

Pairing: Sparkling Wine

INGREDIENTS

½ cup unsalted butter, softened
¼ cup sugar
2⅓ cups all-purpose flour, divided
15 caramels
1½ tablespoons heavy cream
½ cup hazelnuts, raw or roasted,
   roughly chopped
1 cup dried apricots,
   roughly chopped
2 large eggs
1 teaspoon vanilla extract
1 cup light brown sugar, packed
2 tablespoons orange zest
½ teaspoon baking powder
¼ teaspoon salt

1 Preheat oven to 350° F. Lightly butter the bottom and sides of an 8-by-8-inch baking pan. Set aside. In a medium bowl, using an electric mixer, cream together butter and sugar until light and fluffy, about 3 minutes. Mix in 1 cup flour. Beat until just incorporated. Spread dough evenly in the bottom of dish. Bake for 15 minutes. Remove from oven and set aside to cool.

2 Place caramels and heavy cream in a bowl in a microwave oven. Set on high for 45 seconds. Stir, then set on high for an additional 30 seconds. Stir again; caramel should melt to a smooth consistency. (If not, set on high for an additional 15 seconds and stir.)

3 Sprinkle hazelnuts and apricots onto cookie base in pan. Drizzle the caramel mixture over the dried apricots and hazelnuts.

4 In a large bowl, mix together eggs, vanilla and brown sugar. Stir in the orange zest.

5 In a separate bowl, whisk together the remaining 1⅓ cups flour, baking powder and salt. Beat into the brown sugar mixture until just incorporated. The consistency will be between a dough and a batter. Spread over the caramel mixture.

6 Bake for 35-45 minutes. Test with a knife in the center of top dough. It should be moist, not doughy; the edges will be bubbled, not dry. Let rest for 60 minutes before serving. Cut into 1-inch squares.

Yields about 5 dozen

AMUSE
White chocolate, coconut and fresh basil

A mirage where sweetness courts savory, *Amuse* features the chocolate that's not quite a chocolate and yet everything is as bright as it seems. Creamy paired with a crunch, this treat is designed to titillate the taste buds while putting the mind into relaxation mode.

Pairing: Pouilly-Fuissé

INGREDIENTS

½ cup unsalted butter, softened
¾ cup sugar
1 large egg white
½ teaspoon coconut extract
4 ounces white chocolate, melted
1¼ cups all-purpose flour
½ teaspoon baking soda
½ teaspoon baking powder
¼ teaspoon salt
3 tablespoons fresh basil,
 roughly chopped

1 Preheat oven to 350° F. In a large bowl, using an electric mixer, cream together butter and sugar until light and fluffy, about 3 minutes. Mix in egg white, coconut extract and melted white chocolate. Beat until well blended.

2 Whisk together flour, baking soda, baking powder and salt in a small bowl and add to butter mixture. Beat until just incorporated. Fold in chopped basil.

3 Scoop or drop dough by 1 teaspoon portions and place 1½ inches apart on a parchment-lined or nonstick baking sheet. Bake for 7-9 minutes or until bottoms begin to brown. Let sit for a few minutes and transfer to a cooling rack.

Yields about 3 dozen

Shopping List

EMPTY NEST
Banana, cardamom and dried chili

Beyond its role as a cereal topping or the base for a banana split, this tropical fruit can satisfy even the most grown-up craving. *Empty Nest* dresses up bananas with a little tang and heat. This soft, delicious cookie begins with familiar flavor, and then the unexpected kicks in. These cookies are the perfect treat to bring to a gathering at a neighbor's house.

Pairing: Single Malt Whiskey

1 Preheat oven to 325° F. In a large bowl, using an electric mixer, cream together butter and sugars until light and fluffy, about 3 minutes. Beat in eggs, 1 at a time, until blended. Mix in bananas, evaporated milk and vanilla. Beat until well blended.

2 Whisk together flour, cardamom, baking powder, baking soda and salt in a small bowl and add to butter mixture. Beat until just incorporated. Refrigerate dough for 1 hour.

3 Scoop or drop dough by 1 teaspoon portions and place 1½ inches apart on a parchment-lined or nonstick baking sheet. Bake for 8-11 minutes or until bottoms are light golden brown. Let sit for a few minutes and transfer to a cooling rack.

4 To make frosting: Mix together butter, confectioners' sugar, cardamom, vanilla and milk until a glaze consistency is reached. Paint glaze on cookies and top each with a few chili flakes.

Yields about 8 dozen

Shopping List

INGREDIENTS

¾ cup unsalted butter, softened
1½ cups light brown sugar, packed
½ cup sugar
2 large eggs
1½ cups bananas (about 3-4), mashed
¾ cup evaporated milk
1 teaspoon vanilla extract
2¾ cups all-purpose flour
1½ teaspoons ground cardamom
1 teaspoon baking powder
1 teaspoon baking soda
¾ teaspoon salt

FOR FROSTING

2 tablespoons unsalted butter, softened
2 cups confectioners' sugar, sifted
¼ teaspoon ground cardamom
  (½ teaspoon for more flavor)
½ teaspoon vanilla extract
¼ cup evaporated milk
1 tablespoon crushed red pepper flakes, dried

INGREDIENTS

½ cup unsalted butter, softened

¾ cup sugar

1 large egg

2 tablespoons orange zest

2 tablespoons orange juice

4 tablespoons black olives,*
   finely chopped

½ teaspoon fennel seeds, crushed

1 tablespoon fennel leaves, chopped
   medium, optional

1½ cups all-purpose flour

½ teaspoon baking soda

1 teaspoon cream of tartar

¼ teaspoon salt

¼ cup sliced black olives

FOR GLAZE

1 cup confectioners' sugar, sifted

1 tablespoon orange zest

2 tablespoons orange juice

—— SMART COOKIE

Any variety of olive tastes great, so use your favorite. To garner maximum olive flavor, avoid using prechopped olives; instead chop them yourself.

INFUSE
Black olive, orange and fennel

I find myself adding olives to a lot of what I cook. Black olives, orange and fennel permeate these cookies to create a unique infusion of taste. Orange is a great counterpart to the olive. Served as a light snack or an appetizer, *Infuse's* complexity makes it a bit of a show-off and a terrific housewarming gift.

Pairing: Vodka Martini

1 Preheat oven to 400° F. In a large bowl, using an electric mixer, cream together butter and sugar until light and fluffy, about 3 minutes. Mix in egg, orange zest and juice, chopped olives, fennel seeds and fennel leaves (if using). Beat until well blended.

2 Whisk together flour, baking soda, cream of tartar and salt in a small bowl and add to butter mixture. Beat until just incorporated.

3 Scoop or drop dough by 1 rounded teaspoon portions and place 1½ inches apart on a parchment-lined or nonstick baking sheet. Place olive slices, intermittently, on cookies and press lightly. Bake for 10-12 minutes or until bottoms are golden brown. Let sit for a few minutes and transfer to a cooling rack.

4 To make glaze: In a small bowl, mix together confectioners' sugar, orange zest and juice until you reach a glaze consistency. Paint glaze onto cooled cookies to coat.

Yields about 3 dozen

Shopping List

CHA-CHA

Dried cherry, oatmeal, cocoa and chipotle pepper

Oatmeal and cocoa are awakened with dried cherries and chipotle pepper. Not too spicy. Not too sweet. *Cha-Cha* is a satisfying crowd-pleaser that will make you want to dust off your dancing shoes. For an extra punch of flavor, substitute black cherry vodka for the water.

Pairing: Cherry Cola

INGREDIENTS

1 cup unsalted butter, softened
1½ cups sugar
1 large egg
¼ cup water
1 teaspoon vanilla extract
1¼ cups all-purpose flour
⅓ cup unsweetened cocoa powder
1 teaspoon chipotle powder
3 cups old-fashioned oats
1 cup semi-sweet chocolate chips
1 cup dried cherries, roughly chopped

1 Preheat oven to 350° F. In a large bowl, using an electric mixer, cream together butter and sugar until light and fluffy, about 3 minutes. Mix in egg, water (or vodka) and vanilla. Beat until well blended.

2 Whisk together flour, cocoa, chipotle powder and oats in a medium bowl and add to butter mixture. Beat until just incorporated. Fold in chocolate chips and cherries.

3 Scoop or drop dough by 1 rounded teaspoon portions and place 1 inch apart on a parchment-lined or nonstick baking sheet. Bake for 11-14 minutes or until bottoms begin to brown. Let sit for a few minutes and transfer to a cooling rack.

Yields about 6 dozen

Shopping List

Whether you're pulling an all-nighter or have insomnia, this chapter's cookies will satisfy your midnight munchies. Once you've tried these flavor combinations, the thought of them may water your taste buds around the clock.

LATE-NIGHT CRAVING
Buttermilk, maple syrup and bacon

Isn't it strange how a brief thought about pancakes can become a true craving at the oddest hour? *Late-Night Craving* satisfies that desire, complete with maple syrup and a chaser of bacon. Plan ahead and freeze a few scoops of this cookie dough for baking at any hour.

Pairing: Milk

1 Preheat oven to 375° F. In a large bowl, using an electric mixer, cream together butter and sugar until light and fluffy, about 3 minutes. Mix in egg, maple syrup and buttermilk. Beat until well blended.

2 Whisk together flour, baking powder, baking soda and salt in a small bowl and add to butter mixture. Beat until just incorporated. Crumble cooked bacon and fold into dough.

3 Scoop or drop dough by 1 rounded tablespoon portions and place 1½ inches apart on a parchment-lined or nonstick baking sheet. Bake for 10-12 minutes or until bottoms are golden brown. Let sit for a few minutes and transfer to a cooling rack.

Yields about 4 dozen

INGREDIENTS

½ cup unsalted butter, softened
¾ cup sugar
1 large egg
1 tablespoon pure maple syrup
½ cup buttermilk
1¾ cups all-purpose flour
½ teaspoon baking powder
1 teaspoon baking soda
½ teaspoon salt
8-12 strips cooked bacon

Preparation: 8 large or 12 medium strips bacon; cooked, drained and cooled

SMART COOKIE
Craving more sweetness? Make buttercream: Mix together 4 tablespoons softened butter, 2 tablespoons pure maple syrup and 1 cup confectioners' sugar, sifted. Frost cookies.

Shopping List

A SWEET MOMENT AND A SALTY TONGUE

Chocolate, caramel and coarse salt

The milk-chocolate, caramel and salt combination brings this dense cookie to a new level. Creamy caramel and coarse salt entice and entertain with each bite. This recipe never fails to evoke, "This is my most favorite cookie ever" comments which is why you'll probably find yourself craving it at 2 a.m.

Pairing: Tawny Port

INGREDIENTS

1 cup unsalted butter, softened
¾ cup sugar
2 cups all-purpose flour
1 teaspoon baking powder
½ teaspoon baking soda
⅓ cup unsweetened cocoa powder
½ cup chopped high-quality
   milk chocolate bar
2 tablespoons milk
30-36 caramels
3 tablespoons heavy cream
2 tablespoons coarse salt

1 Preheat oven to 325° F. In a large bowl, using an electric mixer, cream together butter and sugar until light and fluffy, about 3 minutes.

2 Whisk together flour, baking powder, baking soda and cocoa powder in a medium bowl and add to butter mixture. Beat until just incorporated. Fold in chopped chocolate. Add milk, 1 tablespoon at a time, until dense but not sticky.

3 Shape dough into 1-inch diameter balls and place 1½ inches apart on a parchment-lined or nonstick baking sheet. Bake for 5 minutes. Remove from oven, then using your thumb or a teaspoon, press a small indentation into each. (If you prefer a lot of caramel, deepen the thumbprint with the back of a teaspoon when the cookies come out of the oven.) Continue baking for an additional 10 minutes. The cookies do not brown; they are cake-like. Let sit for a few of minutes and transfer to a cooling rack.

4 In a medium bowl, microwave caramels and heavy cream on high for 30 seconds. Stir, then microwave for an additional 15 seconds or until soft. Place a dollop of caramel into each cookie thumbprint. Sprinkle coarse salt on top of each as desired.

Yields about 3 dozen

Shopping List

DILLICIOUS

Cucumber, fresh dill, Brie cheese and lemon

Dillicious showcases spring flavors in an appetizing combination. Cucumber, amplified with fresh dill, is enveloped in the brightness of lemon and the warmth of Brie then all are spooned onto a thumbprint base. A bit sweet and a little savory, *Dillicious* is a favorite among cucumber lovers and offers a refreshing taste on a warm night.

Pairing: Sauvignon Blanc

1 Preheat oven to 350° F. In a large bowl, using an electric mixer, cream together butter and sugar until light and fluffy, about 3 minutes. Mix in egg yolks, lemon zest and juice and dill. Beat until well blended.

2 Whisk together flour, baking powder and salt in a small bowl and add to butter mixture. Beat until just incorporated. Refrigerate dough for 30 minutes.

3 Scoop dough by 1½ teaspoon portions, shape into balls and place 1½ inches apart on a parchment-lined or nonstick baking sheet. Using your thumb or a teaspoon, press a small indentation into each. Bake for 7-9 minutes or until bottoms are just golden. Let sit for a few minutes and transfer to a cooling rack.

4 To make topping: In a separate bowl, mix together Brie, cucumber, dill and lemon juice. Spoon about 1 teaspoon cheese mixture into each cookie thumbprint, add more if needed. Refrigerate unserved cookies.

Yields about 3 dozen

Shopping List

INGREDIENTS

1 cup unsalted butter, softened
¾ cup sugar
3 large egg yolks
1 tablespoon lemon zest
2 teaspoons lemon juice
2 tablespoons fresh dill,
  chopped medium
2 cups all-purpose flour
1 teaspoon baking powder
½ teaspoon salt

FOR TOPPING

1 cup Brie cheese, without rind,
  softened
½ cup cucumber, peeled and seeded,
  chopped medium
2 tablespoons fresh dill, chopped
3 tablespoons lemon juice

EYE CANDY

Coconut, white chocolate and pistachio

Crunches of coconut and pistachios come together with a hint of white chocolate in this not-too-sweet coconut macaroon — perfect for the midnight munchies. Simple and fun to make, *Eye Candy* will catch anyone's attention. For best results, use a bar of high-quality white chocolate, not chips.

Pairing: Riesling

INGREDIENTS

¾ cup sugar
2½ cups shredded coconut, sweetened
2 large egg whites, lightly beaten
1 teaspoon vanilla extract
Pinch of salt
½ cup grated high-quality white chocolate
⅓ cup roasted, unsalted pistachio meats, chopped

1 Preheat oven to 325° F. In a large bowl, gently mix together all of the ingredients.

2 Scoop mixture by 1 tablespoon portions, pat together with hands, and place 1 inch apart on a parchment-lined or nonstick baking sheet. Bake for 14-16 minutes or until just golden. Let sit for a few minutes and transfer to a cooling rack. Cool 10 more minutes before serving.

Yields about 2 dozen

Shopping List

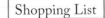

COLLABORATION
Blueberry and sour cream

A shortbread crust is the base for this not-too-sweet bar cookie. Fresh blueberries tame the tang of the sour cream; the taste is creamy and fresh. Delicious at room temperature or straight out of the refrigerator any time a hunger pang strikes.

Pairing: Gewürztraminer

1 Preheat oven to 350° F. Lightly butter the bottom and sides of an 8-by-10-inch baking dish. Set aside. In a large bowl, using an electric mixer, cream together butter and sugar until light and fluffy, about 3 minutes. Mix in vanilla.

2 Whisk together flour and salt in a small bowl and add to butter mixture. Beat until just incorporated.

3 Press dough into the bottom of prepared pan. Bake for 15 minutes. Remove from oven and set aside.

4 For filling: In a medium bowl, mix together sour cream, sugar, ½ tablespoon flour, egg, salt and cinnamon. Fold in blueberries. Spread mixture over bottom crust.

5 For topping: In a small bowl, mix together butter, almonds and remaining 6 tablespoons flour until crumbly. Sprinkle over blueberry mixture. Bake for 40-45 minutes or until a knife inserted comes out moist, not doughy. Let cool for 15 minutes. Cut into small rectangles before serving. The cookies last longer refrigerated and taste great chilled.

Shopping List

Yields 4 dozen

INGREDIENTS

1 cup unsalted butter, softened
½ cup sugar
2 teaspoons vanilla extract
2 cups all-purpose flour
½ teaspoon salt

FOR FILLING AND TOPPING

½ cup sour cream
⅓ cup sugar
6½ tablespoons all-purpose flour, divided
1 large egg, stirred
½ teaspoon salt
½ teaspoon ground cinnamon
1 cup fresh blueberries
¼ cup unsalted butter, cold and cut into small cubes
⅓ cup almonds, chopped medium

DÉJÀ VU

Hazelnut, cream and honey

Nuts, cream and honey — those are the flavors of desserts I loved as a child. *Déjà Vu* is a simple combination of ingredients that warms the heart and reminds me of when baked treats weren't something you bought in a store.

Pairing: Ice Wine

INGREDIENTS

¾ cup unsalted butter, softened
¾ cup sugar
¼ cup light brown sugar, packed
2 large eggs
1 teaspoon vanilla extract
2 teaspoons honey
2¼ cups all-purpose flour
½ teaspoon baking soda
1 teaspoon salt
2 cups hazelnuts, chopped medium

FOR FROSTING AND DECORATION

2 tablespoons unsalted butter, softened
1 cup confectioners' sugar, sifted
2 teaspoons honey (1 tablespoon for a bolder taste)
1-2 tablespoons heavy cream
¼ cup hazelnuts, chopped medium

1 Preheat oven to 350° F. In a large bowl, using an electric mixer, cream together butter and sugars until light and fluffy, about 3 minutes. Beat in eggs, 1 at a time, until blended. Mix in vanilla and honey.

2 Whisk together flour, baking soda and salt in a small bowl and add to butter mixture. Beat until just incorporated. Fold in chopped hazelnuts.

3 Scoop or drop dough by 1 rounded tablespoon portions and place 1½ inches apart on a parchment-lined or nonstick baking sheet. Bake for 10-12 minutes or until bottoms are golden brown. Let sit for a few minutes and transfer to a cooling rack.

4 In a separate bowl, mix together butter, confectioners' sugar, honey and 1 tablespoon heavy cream until a creamy, frosting consistency is reached. Add an additional tablespoon of cream if needed. Frost cookies and sprinkle with chopped hazelnuts.

Yields about 4 dozen

Shopping List

GOOD MORNING

Dried blueberry, coffee, sour cream and brown sugar

The first thing I learned to bake was coffee cake. I'm guessing I was about five years old when I started using my mom's tin pastry cutter to chip cold butter, cinnamon and sugar into small peas. With focus, (eventually) came finesse. The *Good Morning* cookie is a rendition of that softly-sweet coffee cake, with a blueberry and traditional brown-sugar topping. *Good Morning* is a treat for any time of day or night.

Pairing: Latte

1 Soak dried blueberries in 1 cup hot brewed coffee. Set aside.

2 Preheat oven to 350° F. In a large bowl, using an electric mixer, cream together butter and sugar until light and fluffy, about 3 minutes. Mix in egg, vanilla, sour cream and remaining ⅓ cup coffee. Beat until well blended.

3 Whisk together flour, baking soda and salt in a small bowl and add to butter mixture. Beat until just incorporated. Drain coffee from dried blueberries. Fold blueberries into the mixture.

4 To make topping: In a separate bowl, cut cold butter into small pea-sized pieces. Stir in flour, brown sugar and cinnamon. Set aside.

5 Scoop or drop dough by 1 rounded teaspoon portions, roll into balls, and place 1½ inches apart on a parchment-lined or nonstick baking sheet. Press each to ¼ inch-thickness. Sprinkle about ½ teaspoon topping mixture onto each cookie. Bake for 9-11 minutes or until bottoms are golden brown. Let sit for a few minutes and transfer to a cooling rack.

Shopping List

Yields about 4 dozen

INGREDIENTS

1 cup dried blueberries
1⅓ cups hot brewed coffee, divided
½ cup unsalted butter, softened
1 cup light brown sugar, packed
1 large egg
1 teaspoon vanilla extract
¾ cup sour cream
2¼ cups all-purpose flour
½ teaspoon baking soda
½ teaspoon salt

FOR TOPPING

¼ cup unsalted butter, cold
¼ cup all-purpose flour
½ cup light brown sugar, packed
¾ teaspoon ground cinnamon

ALTER EGO

Honey, cumin, cayenne pepper, salt and pepper

This cookie pays homage to one of my son's favorite store-bought, spicy tortilla chips. Fun to make, *Alter Ego* entertains the senses with bold flavors and an attitude that shouts hot, sweet and salty all at once — terrific when served with beer, alongside appetizers or as a dessert after a barbecue.

Pairing: Amber Ale

INGREDIENTS

¼ cup butter, unsalted or salted
¼ cup honey
½ cup confectioners' sugar, sifted
½ teaspoon cumin
¼ teaspoon cayenne pepper
¼ teaspoon coarse salt
¼ teaspoon coarsely ground black
   pepper
2 tablespoons cornmeal
2 tablespoons all-purpose flour

1 Preheat oven to 350° F. Line a rimmed cookie sheet with parchment paper. In a medium bowl, microwave butter and honey for 30-40 seconds, until melted together. Stir occasionally. Do not let boil. Whisk in sugar, cumin, cayenne, salt and black pepper until smooth.

2 Whisk in cornmeal and flour until just incorporated. Spread batter to within 1 inch of the cookie sheet edges. (It does not need to be perfectly even.)

3 Bake for 13-15 minutes. The cookies are done when bubbly and medium browned. Cool 2 minutes, then slide cookie and parchment paper onto a cutting board. After 2 more minutes, use a sharp knife to slice cookies into desired shapes; leave on the parchment paper and cutting board to cool for an additional 3-5 minutes. (If the cookies start to break up when cutting, they are a little too cool. Place back into the oven for 1 minute to soften and then repeat the cutting process.) Peel from paper or cutting board and place on a cooling rack or plate.

Yields about 3 dozen

Shopping List

REALLY?
Kalamata olive and white chocolate

Yes, really. These juxtaposed flavors confuse the palate for a brief moment then delight the taste buds with their unusual duet. Use a high-quality white chocolate for this recipe. Roughly chop the olives and white chocolate or — daringly — leave both in larger chunks. Prepared either way, *Really?* is a tasteful surprise for late-night conversations; an odd cookie for odd moments.

Pairing: Pinot Noir

1. Preheat oven to 375° F. In a large bowl, using an electric mixer, cream together butter and sugars until light and fluffy, about 3 minutes. Mix in egg and vanilla. Beat until well blended.

2. Whisk together flour, baking soda and salt in a small bowl and add to butter mixture. Beat until just incorporated. Mix in chocolate and olives.

3. Scoop or drop dough by 1 teaspoon portions and place 1½ inches apart on a parchment-lined or nonstick baking sheet. Bake for 8-9 minutes or until bottoms are just golden. Let sit for a few minutes and transfer to a cooling rack.

Yields about 7 dozen

INGREDIENTS

1 cup unsalted butter, softened
¾ cup sugar
¾ cup light brown sugar, packed
1 large egg
1 teaspoon vanilla extract
2¼ cups all-purpose flour
1 teaspoon baking soda
1 teaspoon salt
1 (4.4-ounce) high-quality white chocolate bar, roughly chopped (yield about 1 cup)
½ cup kalamata olives, roughly chopped

Shopping List

CAPTIVATING

Jalapeno pepper, fresh mint and dark chocolate

I always enjoy stuffed jalapeno appetizers and decided this cookie version is yet another way to keep the night sizzling long after dinner. *Captivating* will turn your taste buds inside out. It's a cookie baked into one half of a jalapeno, which is first lined with fresh mint and dark chocolate. Jalapeno and cookie fans agree — it's captivating!

Pairing: Mojito

INGREDIENTS

½ cup unsalted butter, softened
⅔ cup sugar
1 large egg
1½ teaspoons vanilla extract
1½ cups all-purpose flour
¼ teaspoon baking powder
¼ teaspoon baking soda
¼ teaspoon salt
18 jalapeno peppers, seeded and halved
1 tablespoon olive oil
2 tablespoons fresh mint leaves, roughly chopped
8 ounces high-quality dark chocolate, broken into ¼-inch squares

1 Preheat oven to 350° F. In a large bowl, using an electric mixer, cream together butter and sugar until light and fluffy, about 3 minutes. Mix in egg and vanilla. Beat until well blended.

2 Whisk together flour, baking powder, baking soda and salt in a small bowl and add to butter mixture. Beat until just incorporated.

3 Line a cookie sheet with parchment paper or aluminum foil. Place each jalapeno half on sheet, about 1½ inches apart. If needed, in order for each pepper half to rest flat, level by lightly shaving the underside in one spot. If the jalapeno tips during baking, the cookie dough will spill out. Using a dab of olive oil, lightly wipe the outside of the jalapeno, where it will rest on the cookie sheet.

4 Place 3 pieces of mint leaves into each jalapeno half. Then place 3 squares of chocolate over mint leaves. Scoop or drop dough by 1 teaspoon portions; using hands, roll to the length of a jalapeno half. Tuck dough into the pepper over the mint and chocolate. Remove any dough that overfills the pepper. Place an additional piece of chocolate, lengthwise, into the dough so half of the chocolate is still showing. Bake for 9-11 minutes or until just golden. Let sit for 5 minutes and transfer to a cooling rack.

Yields about 3 dozen

Shopping List

A FLAVOR TANGO

Cornmeal, lemon and cayenne pepper

Just when you think the flavor of this lemon-and-cornmeal cookie is nearly gone from your mouth, cayenne pepper unexpectedly flickers along the sides of your tongue. Skeptics become converts after trying a few bites. *A Flavor Tango* freezes well and is a great take-anywhere (or anytime) cookie.

Pairing: Sparkling Shiraz

1 Preheat oven to 375° F. In a large bowl, using an electric mixer, cream together butter and sugar until light and fluffy, about 3 minutes. Mix in egg, lemon zest and juice. Beat until well blended.

2 Whisk together flour, cornmeal, baking powder, salt and cayenne pepper in a small bowl and add to butter mixture. Beat until just incorporated.

3 Scoop or drop dough by 1 rounded teaspoon portions, roll into balls, and place 1½ inches apart on a parchment-lined or nonstick baking sheet. Bake for 12 minutes or until bottoms are golden brown. Let sit for a few minutes and transfer to a cooling rack.

Yields about 3 dozen

INGREDIENTS

½ cup unsalted butter, softened
⅔ cup sugar
1 large egg
2 tablespoons lemon zest
2 tablespoons lemon juice
1 cup all-purpose flour
½ cup cornmeal
1 teaspoon baking powder
½ teaspoon coarse salt
1 teaspoon cayenne pepper

Shopping List

CLASSIC

Vanilla, cocoa powder and mint

Can't get to sleep? Slice and bake these cookies in the middle of the night but first play with the dough a bit to create a visual accent or two. One dough, two interpretations. A simple cookie, *Classic* helps you forget the countless commercials airing on late-night TV or tomorrow morning's irritating commute.

Pairing: Baileys Irish Cream on Ice

INGREDIENTS

1 cup, plus 2 tablespoons, unsalted butter, softened

1 cup sugar

1 large egg, plus 1 egg yolk

2½ cups all-purpose flour

¾ teaspoon baking powder

½ teaspoon salt

½ teaspoon mint extract

1 teaspoon lemon juice

3 ounces high-quality dark chocolate, melted

½ teaspoon vanilla extract

½ teaspoon ground cinnamon

1 In a large bowl, using an electric mixer, cream together butter and sugar until light and fluffy, about 3 minutes. Mix in egg and egg yolk. Beat until well blended.

2 Whisk together flour, baking powder and salt in a small bowl and add to butter mixture. Beat until just incorporated. Divide mixture evenly into 2 bowls.

3 In one bowl, add mint extract and lemon juice to dough and mix on low speed until incorporated.

4 In a small separate bowl, stir together melted chocolate, vanilla and cinnamon. In remaining bowl of dough, add chocolate mixture to second half of dough and mix on low speed until incorporated. Form each portion of dough into 1 log (1½ inches in diameter) and wrap each in parchment paper. Freeze for 1 hour or refrigerate for 3 hours.

Shopping List

5 Preheat oven to 350° F. Slice logs into ¼-inch-thick rounds and place 1 inch apart on a parchment-lined or nonstick baking sheet. For decoration, add small accents of dough from one kind of dough to the other, as you like. The accents can be small balls pressed onto a cookie, or small shapes of ⅛-inch-thick dough slices. (See photo.) Bake for 9-11 minutes or until bottoms are light golden brown. Let sit for a few minutes and transfer to a cooling rack.

Yields about 4 dozen

Chapter 9

I'll Think About That Tomorrow

After a long, arduous day, you deserve to pause, exhale and take time for yourself. *Cookies for Grown-ups* honors all that you do and hopes these treats provide reason to take a break from your "to-do" list. Relax and savor great tastes before jumping back into the fire.

CRAVE
White chocolate and espresso; milk chocolate and vanilla

The fun shapes of these crisp, chocolate-frosted cookies appeal to your inner child while their taste satisfies the sweet tooth you still have. *Crave* is perfect when you're craving a respite from a long project or when a free weekend finally arrives.

Pairing: Coffee

1 In a large bowl, using an electric mixer, cream together butter and sugar until light and fluffy, about 3 minutes. Mix in egg. Beat until well blended.

2 Whisk together flour and salt in a small bowl and add to butter mixture. Beat until just incorporated.

3 Form dough into a 1½-inch square log and wrap in parchment paper. Freeze for 1 hour or refrigerate for 2 hours.

4 Preheat oven to 350° F. Cut log into ⅛-inch-thick slices and cut each into odd bite-sized shapes. With the trim pieces, create small, bite-sized balls. Arrange slices and balls 1 inch apart on a parchment-lined or nonstick baking sheet. Bake for 11-13 minutes or until bottoms are just golden. Let sit for a few minutes and transfer to a cooling rack.

5 To make frosting (A): Microwave white chocolate in a small bowl, in 20-second intervals, typically 3-4 times, stirring in between each until smooth. Add butter, confectioners' sugar and espresso. Stir into a creamy frosting consistency. In a separate bowl, repeat for frosting (B). Using a combination of the two flavors, lightly frost flat cookies and dip rounded cookies into frosting. Let set for about 10 minutes before serving.

Yields about 5 dozen (bite-sized cookies)

Shopping List

INGREDIENTS

¾ cup unsalted butter, softened
¾ cup confectioners' sugar, sifted
1 large egg
1½ cups all-purpose flour
¼ teaspoon salt

FOR FROSTING (A)

2 ounces high-quality white chocolate
2 tablespoons unsalted butter, softened
1 cup confectioners' sugar, sifted
2 tablespoons espresso*

FROSTING (B)

2 ounces high-quality milk chocolate
2 tablespoons unsalted butter, softened
1 cup confectioners' sugar, sifted
½ teaspoon vanilla extract
2 tablespoons milk

—— SMART COOKIE

*If coffee doesn't appeal to you, substitute ½ teaspoon maple extract and 2 tablespoons milk in place of the espresso.

KATHY
Banana, rum and walnut

My cousin Kathy and I were inseparable as girls, as evidenced by our many bike trips where she pedaled and I rode on the bumper or the handlebars. As a young cook, she also made the best banana-nut bread. Kathy lives in Tennessee now and we rarely get together but when we do we still laugh about how she was always the one pedaling. This cookie pays homage to her and that wonderful bread. Enjoy this treat during an afternoon break.

Pairing: Hot Tea

INGREDIENTS

3 tablespoons light brown sugar, packed

1 cup bananas, sliced into ¼-inch rounds

1 tablespoon rum

½ cup, plus 2 tablespoons, unsalted butter, softened, divided

1 cup sugar

1 large egg

1 teaspoon vanilla extract

2¼ cups all-purpose flour

1 teaspoon cream of tartar

1 teaspoon baking soda

¼ teaspoon salt

¾ cup walnuts, chopped medium

1 Preheat oven to 350° F. Place brown sugar on a plate, lightly press banana slices in brown sugar, so there is a light amount of sugar on each side. Melt rum and 2 tablespoons butter in a medium pan over low heat, sauté banana slices for about 2 minutes on each side to caramelize. Set aside.

2 In a large bowl, using an electric mixer, cream together remaining ½ cup butter and sugar until light and fluffy, about 3 minutes. Mix in egg and vanilla. Beat until well blended.

3 Whisk together flour, cream of tartar, baking soda and salt in a small bowl and add to butter mixture. Beat until just incorporated. Lightly mash sautéed bananas. Stir bananas and walnuts into dough.

4 Scoop or drop dough by 1 rounded teaspoon portions and place 1½ inches apart on a parchment-lined or nonstick baking sheet. Bake for 7-9 minutes or until bottoms are golden brown. Let sit for a few minutes and transfer to a cooling rack.

Yields about 5 dozen

Shopping List

QUENCH
Mandarin orange and dark chocolate

Quench satisfies with a burst of mandarin orange, blanketed in cookie, frosted in chocolate, topped off with a morsel of dark chocolate. The moist smoky flavor of the mandarin orange, soft crunch of cookie and bite of chocolate will quench all of your desires. Well, perhaps that's a bit of an exaggeration. Let's just say savoring a snack of *Quench* is a great way to put off obligations for an hour or two.

Pairing: Merlot

1. In a large bowl, using an electric mixer, cream together butter and sugars until light and fluffy, about 3 minutes. Mix in egg and vanilla. Beat until well blended.

2. Whisk together flour, ginger, baking soda and salt in a small bowl and add to butter mixture. Beat until just incorporated. Refrigerate dough for 30 minutes.

3. Preheat oven to 325° F. Scoop or drop dough by 1 teaspoon portions and flatten each to an oval with ¼-inch thickness. Drape an oval of dough over each orange section, and gently fold dough around the orange on three sides, leaving just a bit of orange visible. Place 1½ inches apart on a parchment-lined or nonstick baking sheet. Bake for 9-11 minutes or until bottoms are golden brown. Let sit for a few minutes and transfer to a cooling rack.

4. To make frosting: In a separate bowl, mix together butter, confectioners' sugar, cocoa powder, vanilla and milk, and stir to a creamy frosting consistency, adding a touch more milk as needed. Frost the top of each cookie. Then place a square of chocolate on each.

Shopping List

Yields about 2 dozen

INGREDIENTS

½ cup unsalted butter, softened
1½ cups sugar
¼ cup light brown sugar, packed
1 large egg
1 teaspoon vanilla extract
1½ cups all-purpose flour
¼ teaspoon ground ginger
½ teaspoon baking soda
¼ teaspoon salt
12 sections of fresh mandarin orange, cut in half to yield 24 sections

FOR FROSTING
½ cup unsalted butter, softened
2¼ cups confectioners' sugar, sifted
½ cup cocoa powder
¼ teaspoon vanilla extract
¼ cup milk
24 (¼-inch) squares high-quality dark chocolate

INGREDIENTS

½ cup unsalted butter, softened
¾ cup sugar
1 large egg
1½ cups all-purpose flour
1 teaspoon cream of tartar
½ teaspoon baking soda
¼ teaspoon salt
¼ cup hazelnuts, chopped medium
1 teaspoon ground cinnamon
1 tablespoon sugar
¼ cup shredded coconut, toasted

FOR FRUIT PREPARATION AND ASSEMBLY

72 pieces/slices of fruit* (I use 2 bananas,
    6 strawberries and ¼ pineapple)
2 tablespoons unsalted butter, softened
2 tablespoons light brown sugar, packed

Special equipment: 2 dozen (6-inch)
    wooden skewers

SMART COOKIE

*Use your preference of fruit.
Fruit should not be overripe; any
combination works well.*

SWEET KEBAB

Strawberry, pineapple, banana, hazelnut, coconut and cinnamon

Sweet Kebab is a tasty way to spend creative time in the kitchen. One dough is divided into thirds then each third is rolled in either chopped nuts, toasted coconut or cinnamon and sugar. Each cookie is threaded onto a skewer, divided by caramelized strawberry, pineapple or banana. *Sweet Kebab* is simultaneously sweet, tart, soft and crunchy — a powerhouse of flavors and textures.

Pairing: Sauvignon Blanc

1 In a large bowl, using an electric mixer, cream together butter and sugar until light and fluffy, about 3 minutes. Mix in egg. Beat until well blended.

2 Whisk together flour, cream of tartar, baking soda and salt in a small bowl and add to butter mixture. Beat until just incorporated. Refrigerate dough for 30 minutes.

3 Preheat oven to 400° F. Scoop or drop dough by 1 rounded teaspoon portions. Shape into balls. Roll ⅓ of the balls into chopped hazelnuts. Stir together the cinnamon and sugar, and roll ⅓ of the balls in cinnamon-sugar mixture. Then roll remaining balls in toasted coconut. Place each ball 1½ inches apart on a parchment-lined or nonstick baking sheet. Bake for 10-12 minutes or until bottoms are golden brown. Let sit for a few minutes and transfer to a cooling rack.

Shopping List

4 To prepare fruit: Cut fruit into equal portions. Melt butter and brown sugar over medium heat in a large sauté pan or skillet. Toss fruit pieces in mixture, gently stirring, for 2 minutes to lightly coat in mixture until fruit begins to caramelize. Set aside.

5 Each kebab will consist of one each of the three types of cookies you've baked (hazelnut, cinnamon, coconut), alternated with one of your fruit selections. (If using three kinds of fruit, then use a piece of each on every skewer.) To assemble: Delicately turn the skewer to pierce each item at its center then carefully move it up the stick.

Yields about 2 dozen kebab skewers

INGREDIENTS

1 cup unsalted butter, softened

1 cup sugar

1 large egg

1 (4.4-ounce) high-quality white
 chocolate bar, grated or finely
 chopped

1 teaspoon fresh ginger root, minced

1 teaspoon lemon zest

2½ cups all-purpose flour

½ cup shredded coconut, toasted

¼ teaspoon baking powder

¼ teaspoon salt

⅓ cup fresh raspberries, quartered*

⅔ cup fresh blueberries, halved*

———— SMART COOKIE ————

Other berries may be substituted, such as blackberries or strawberries. For drier berries, use ⅔ cup for each berry (I used only ⅓ cup raspberries, as they can be very moist). If you find the berries make the dough too wet, add an additional ¼ cup coconut to that half of the dough. Alternatively, you can mix in berries together rather than divide dough in half as above.

BERRY BASKET
Berry, white chocolate, fresh ginger and coconut

Berry Basket is reminiscent of a hearty store-bought cookie my mom and I ate when I was a kid. We liked to eat the cookie with fruit, ice cream or both. Berry Basket's refreshing flavors are a great morning treat. The cookies are also perfect in a picnic basket or lunchbox.

Pairing: Sweet Riesling

1 In a large bowl, using an electric mixer, cream together butter and sugar until light and fluffy, about 3 minutes. Mix in egg, white chocolate, ginger and lemon zest. Beat until well blended.

2 Whisk together flour, coconut, baking powder and salt in a small bowl and add to butter mixture. Beat until just incorporated. Divide dough in half, place one half in separate bowl.

3 Gently fold raspberries into half of dough. In the bowl with remaining half of dough, gently fold in blueberries. Place each half of dough on a separate piece of parchment paper. Shape each into a 2-inch-wide by ½-inch-high rectangle. Wrap and freeze for 30-60 minutes or refrigerate for 3-4 hours.

4 Preheat oven to 375° F. Peel away parchment paper from each rectangle. Stack the two halves of dough. Slice stacked dough into ¼-inch-thick rectangles and place 1½ inches apart on a parchment-lined or nonstick baking sheet. Bake for 10-12 minutes or until bottoms are light golden brown. Let sit for a few minutes and transfer to a cooling rack.

Yields about 3 dozen

Shopping List

FLAVOR POCKET
Pear, agave nectar and Cheddar cheese

Fast forward to cocktail hour, tomorrow is another day, a day when *Flavor Pocket* will be served with apéritifs. Pear complements the cheese tucked with it into layers of buttery dough. D'Anjou pears work beautifully with sharp Cheddar.

Pairing: Champagne Cocktail

1 In a large bowl, using an electric mixer, cream together cream cheese, sugar and 1 cup butter until light and fluffy, about 3 minutes. Mix in vanilla. Beat until well blended.

2 Whisk together flour and salt in a small bowl and add to butter mixture. Beat until just incorporated.

3 Form dough into 2 logs (1½ inches in diameter) and wrap each in parchment paper. Freeze for 1 hour or refrigerate for 2 hours.

4 Halve the pears and slice thinly. Melt remaining 2 tablespoons butter with agave nectar in a medium saucepan over medium-low heat; gently sauté pear slices turning once, about 30 seconds on each side to coat with mixture. If the pears are under ripe, you may need 1 minute for each side. Set aside.

5 Preheat oven to 350° F. Cut logs into ⅛-inch-thick slices and place 1½ inches apart on a parchment-lined or nonstick baking sheet. Place a square of cheese and a slice of pear on each slice. Cut additional pieces of the sliced dough in half and place a half over each cookie. No need to mold the top half circle to the bottom full circle, the dough will form nicely during baking. Do not handle the top half too much, as it may result in a cracked top. Bake for 13-15 minutes or until bottoms are golden brown. Let sit for a few minutes and transfer to a cooling rack.

Yields about 3 dozen

INGREDIENTS

1 cup, plus 2 tablespoons, unsalted butter, softened, divided
3 ounces cream cheese
½ cup sugar
1 tablespoon vanilla extract
2 cups all-purpose flour
½ teaspoon salt
2 pears, preferably D'Anjou or Bosc varieties, cored and unpeeled
2 tablespoons agave nectar (or honey)
About 36 (½-inch squares) sharp Cheddar cheese slices

Shopping List

EXPLORE
Caramel, orange and hazelnut

The flavor-intense orange and hazelnut base of the *Explore* cookie is wonderfully complemented by its brown butter frosting.

Pairing: Irish Coffee

INGREDIENTS

½ cup unsalted butter, softened
¾ cup sugar
1 large egg
1 teaspoon orange juice
1⅔ cups all-purpose flour
½ teaspoon baking powder
¼ teaspoon salt
½ cup hazelnuts, chopped medium

FOR BROWN BUTTER FROSTING

¼ cup unsalted butter, softened
½ cup light brown sugar, packed
¼ cup, plus 3 tablespoons, heavy cream, divided
1 teaspoon orange juice
½ teaspoon vanilla extract
2 cups confectioners' sugar, sifted

1. In a large bowl, using an electric mixer, cream together butter and sugar until light and fluffy, about 3 minutes. Mix in egg and orange juice. Beat until well blended.

2. Whisk together flour, baking powder and salt in a small bowl and add to butter mixture. Beat until just incorporated. Fold in hazelnuts. Refrigerate dough for 1 hour.

3. Preheat oven to 350° F. Scoop or drop dough by 1 teaspoon portions, shape into balls, and flatten each to ¼ inch-thickness with fingers. Place the cookies 1 inch apart on a parchment-lined or nonstick baking sheet. Bake for 11-13 minutes or until bottoms are golden brown. Let sit for a few minutes and transfer to a cooling rack.

4. To make frosting: Melt butter in small, heavy skillet over low heat; bring butter to a soft boil, stirring constantly. Stir in brown sugar; continue to stir at a low boil for 2 minutes. Stir in 3 tablespoons heavy cream; continue to stir at a low boil for 4 minutes. Place mixture into a medium bowl. Using an electric mixer, add orange juice, vanilla, confectioners' sugar and remaining ¼ cup heavy cream. Mix at high speed for 2-3 minutes, until creamy. Frost cookies.

Yields about 3 dozen

Shopping List

STICKY RICE

Rice, mango and coconut milk

Forget about the rest of today, travel to another place with this cookie. Think sticky rice, tropical mangoes and coconuts. Are we there yet? *Sticky Rice* offers a soft morsel and a surprising texture for the palate. Since authentic sweet rice is difficult to find, this recipe is based on grocery-store jasmine rice. It's a taste-traveling experience.

Pairing: Thai Iced Tea

1. In a large bowl, using an electric mixer, cream together butter and sugar until light and fluffy, about 3 minutes.

2. Whisk together flour and salt in a small bowl and add to butter mixture. Beat until just incorporated. Mix in coconut milk, mango and jasmine rice on low speed. Refrigerate dough for 1 hour.

3. Preheat oven to 375° F. Scoop or drop dough by 1 teaspoon portions and place 1½ inches apart on a parchment-lined or nonstick baking sheet. Bake for 10-12 minutes or until bottoms are golden brown. Let sit for a few minutes and transfer to a cooling rack.

4. To make glaze: Mix together mango, butter, confectioners' sugar and coconut milk to a consistency between a frosting and glaze. Place a small amount of glaze onto the top of each cookie.

Yields about 5 dozen

Shopping List

INGREDIENTS

½ cup unsalted butter, softened
1¾ cups confectioners' sugar, sifted
1½ cups all-purpose flour
½ teaspoon salt
⅔ cup coconut milk
½ cup mashed mango
2 cups cooked jasmine rice

FOR GLAZE

¼ cup mashed mango
1 tablespoon unsalted butter, softened
1½ cups confectioners' sugar, sifted
2-3 tablespoons coconut milk

SMART COOKIE

Get prepared: You'll need two cups of cooked jasmine rice for this recipe. If you have leftover jasmine rice in the fridge, use that or make it in advance.

SOUTHERN TANG
Apple and dried cranberry

My grandma, Bertha, hailed from North Carolina so I grew up on biscuits topped with homemade applesauce for breakfast. *Southern Tang* is the cookie version of that early-morning treat I so fondly remember, though slightly sweeter and studded with dried cranberries. Use whichever apple variety is your favorite. Put off those weekend chores a little while longer by starting with a relaxing morning and a plate of *Southern Tang*.

Pairing: Iced Tea

INGREDIENTS

½ cup, plus 2 tablespoons, unsalted butter, softened, divided
2 cups Granny Smith apples, pared, peeled and roughly chopped
⅓ cup water
¾ cup, plus 1 tablespoon, sugar, divided
2 tablespoons shortening
1 large egg
1 teaspoon vanilla extract
⅓ cup cold buttermilk
2 cups all-purpose flour
½ teaspoon baking powder
¼ teaspoon baking soda
½ teaspoon salt
¾ cup dried cranberries

1 Preheat oven to 325° F. Melt 2 tablespoons butter in a medium saucepan over medium heat, sauté apples for about 2 minutes. Add water and 1 tablespoon sugar and bring to a low boil, then simmer for 10-15 minutes or until apples are soft but not mushy. Remove from heat. Drain any remaining water. Set aside.

2 In a large bowl, using an electric mixer, cream together shortening, remaining ½ cup butter and ¾ cup sugar until light and fluffy, about 3 minutes. Mix in egg, vanilla and buttermilk until well blended.

3 Whisk together flour, baking powder, baking soda and salt in a small bowl and add to butter mixture. Beat until just incorporated. Fold in cranberries.

4 Scoop or drop dough by 1 rounded teaspoon portions, shape into balls and place 1½ inches apart on a parchment-lined or nonstick baking sheet. Using your thumb or a teaspoon, press a small indentation into each. Bake for 11-13 minutes or until bottoms are golden brown. Let sit for a few minutes and transfer to a cooling rack.

Shopping List

5 When cool, spoon about 1-1½ teaspoons applesauce mixture into each cookie thumbprint. If you do not plan to serve cookies immediately, refrigerate applesauce and spoon onto cookies just before serving. Or, heat the applesauce before spooning onto cookies.

Yields about 4 dozen

NOSH

Dry roasted peanut, dried chili and fresh cilantro

Turn off your phone, put up your feet and chill. *Nosh* is an addictive cookie that'll take your mind away from responsibilities until another day. It pairs perfectly with beer, peanuts and television. Dried chili flakes and cilantro will keep you awake enough to eat several and have a second beer.

Pairing: Amber Ale

INGREDIENTS

½ cup unsalted butter, softened
½ cup sugar
½ cup light brown sugar, packed
1 large egg
½ teaspoon vanilla extract
2 tablespoons fresh cilantro,
    finely chopped
1 cup all-purpose flour
2 cups dry-roasted salted peanuts
2 tablespoons dried chili flakes
    (reduce if you prefer a milder flavor)
1 teaspoon baking powder
1½ teaspoons coarse salt

1 In a large bowl, using an electric mixer, cream together butter and sugars until light and fluffy, about 3 minutes. Mix in egg, vanilla and cilantro. Beat until well blended.

2 Whisk together flour, peanuts, chili flakes, baking powder and salt in a small bowl and add to butter mixture. Beat until just incorporated. Refrigerate dough for 1 hour.

3 Preheat oven to 350° F. Scoop or drop dough by 1 teaspoon portions, sprinkle each with a pinch of coarse salt and place 1½ inches apart on a parchment-lined or nonstick baking sheet. Bake for 9-11 minutes or until bottoms are golden brown. Let sit for a few minutes and transfer to a cooling rack.

Yields about 4 dozen

Shopping List

VENEZIA

Mozzarella cheese, fresh basil and tomato

A cross between ravioli and a Margherita pizza, *Venezia* is a soft, savory cookie that inspires wanderlust. Can you already picture yourself stepping onto a gondola? There's no better way to put things off for a while than to plan your next holiday.

Pairing: Zinfandel

1 In a large bowl, using an electric mixer, cream together butter and sugar until light and fluffy, about 3 minutes. Mix in egg and orange juice. Beat until well blended.

2 Whisk together flour, baking soda and salt in a small bowl and add to butter mixture. Beat until just incorporated.

3 Form dough into a log (1½ inches in diameter) and wrap in parchment paper. Freeze for 1 hour or refrigerate for 2 hours.

4 Preheat oven to 400° F. Cut log into ⅛-inch-thick slices. Place a piece of basil leaf and a (1-inch) square of mozzarella on each slice of dough, fold the dough around the cheese and pinch the edges creating what will look like a small ravioli or stuffed pasta. Place each seam side down 1½ inches apart on a parchment-lined or nonstick baking sheet; gently flatten the top of each cookie. Then place a (½-inch) square of mozzarella and a tomato slice on top of each.

5 Bake for 8-9 minutes or until bottoms are just golden. (If the tomato or mozzarella on top shifts during baking, move both to the center of the cookie. The cheese and tomato may spread when you do, but the cookie will taste good – you are moving them for appearance only.) Let sit for a few minutes and transfer to a cooling rack.

Yields about 2 dozen

INGREDIENTS

½ cup unsalted butter, softened
½ cup sugar
1 large egg
1 tablespoon orange juice
1½ cups all-purpose flour
½ teaspoon baking soda
¼ teaspoon salt
24 (1-inch) pieces fresh basil leaves
24 (1-inch) squares fresh mozzarella cheese

FOR BAKED-ON TOPPING

24 (½-inch) squares fresh mozzarella cheese
24 (¼-inch) slices ripe cherry or heirloom tomatoes

Shopping List

ACKNOWLEDGMENTS

Hearty, flavorful thanks go to friends and family for tasting and test-baking cookies. Additional thanks go to Donette Dake for the use of her kitchen, the gift of a great mixer and for her wonderful, supportive sense of humor. Thanks also to Veronika Focht for her amazing graphic design talent and enthusiasm to discuss, read and watch all things food-related with me, her mother-in-law. Lastly, thank you Victoria Bartz, for championing my wild ideas and inventions.

Appreciative, respectful thanks go to my agent Regina Ryan, to everyone at Red Rock Press, to my editor Clarke Reilly and book designer Susan Smilanic. Finally, thank you Frank, you're exceptional.

– Kelly

I wish to thank Milva Gobbi of Sur la Table for her styling assistance.

– Frank

Index   Cookies   A to V